Everyday Paleo
around the world

ITALIAN CUISINE

Authentic Recipes Made Gluten-Free

Sarah Fragoso

VICTORY BELT PUBLISHING INC.

Las Vegas

First Published in 2013 by Victory Belt Publishing Inc.

ISBN 13: 978-1-936608-30-0

Printed in the USA

RRD 01-13

Sarah Fragoso is the national bestselling author of *Everyday Paleo* and *Everyday Paleo Family Cookbook,* and she is co-owner of Everyday Paleo Lifestyle and Fitness. For more information on Sarah Fragoso visit: www.everydaypaleo.com

Recipe Photos by: Michael J. Lang www.jcmichaelphotography.com
On Location Photos by: Damon Meledones www.cameradamon.com
Cover Photo by: Steve Twist www.avalonportraits.com
Author Photo by: Shannon Rosan www.shannonrosan.com
Cover Design by: Oxbow Rising

TABLE OF CONTENTS

LET THE ADVENTURE BEGIN!

*W*elcome to *Everyday Paleo Around the World: Italian Cuisine*! This book is much more than *just* Italian recipes made Paleo; it's a resource filled with life lessons that can only be learned when embedded in another culture, a book that will take you on an adventure with us to the beautiful and amazing country of Italy. It represents the beginning of our family's incredible journey around the world.

You might ask, "What does traveling the world have to do with Paleo?" In my opinion, Paleo is so much more than nutrition. It's a way of life and a way of thinking. It's striving for health, which encompasses all aspects of how humans are intended to live. It nurtures body, mind, and spirit. I am so blessed that my career is focused on spreading one simple message: In order to live the best life possible, you must first begin by eating real food.

Eating real food quite literally saved my life and, in return, my only wish is to share with others the good health that I have been given. It might sound crazy to some, but to those who are like me and have regained their health, you know exactly what I'm talking about. When you finally have the energy to make it through your day, when all the ailments that have plagued you (even though you probably thought the long list of problems were just "normal" parts of life) finally dissipate, and when you start to become strong and capable in your own body, it's difficult to keep quiet about your newfound lease on life. Now, five years into my Paleo journey, I'm still sharing, learning, growing, and happy that there is no end to this adventure. In fact, it's only just beginning.

As my children grow they are testaments to this amazing lifestyle. Each passing day is a reassurance that I am meant to continue to share our story about living a Paleo lifestyle and to help others navigate along their own paths to health and wellness. I firmly believe that the Paleo lifestyle can help us all not just survive our way through life, but *thrive*. Now I have the opportunity to take *Everyday Paleo* around the world, and I'm bringing all of you right along with me!

This cookbook is not an introduction to Paleo, but I'll offer a brief explanation of Paleo's tenets. The Paleo plan recommends avoiding grains, dairy, legumes, vegetable oils, and processed sugar while focusing on unprocessed foods such as grass-fed meats, vegetables, fruits, and healthy fats like animal fat, coconut, olive oil, nuts, and seeds. This book is

appropriate for anyone living a Paleo or gluten-free lifestyle. However, if you are brand new to Paleo, I suggest you also read my first book, *Everyday Paleo,* as well as *The Paleo Coach* by Jason Seib. And if you are interested in more of the "science" behind this lifestyle, I also recommend *The Paleo Solution* by Robb Wolf. These books will give you all the information you need to help you begin a healthier, more natural approach to eating.

If you have read my other two books, *Everyday Paleo* and the *Everyday Paleo Family Cookbook,* you've caught a glimpse of who I am. I love to cook, I love to eat, and most of all, I love spending time with my family. My husband and my boys are my greatest gifts in life, and having the energy to play, laugh, explore, and learn alongside them rather than just watch from the sidelines has been the best side effect of eating, moving, and living as humans are intended. Today, the Fragoso family has entered a new chapter.

I find it incredibly important to honor the vast array of different cultures, traditions, and lifestyles, and there is so much we can learn from others outside of our own home base. My own family has many cultural influences, including Spanish, Mexican, Filipino, Irish, Native American, and Portuguese, and all are privileged with amazing cuisine. Part of the joy that I have found when cooking is adapting different traditional ethnic cuisines and making the recipes Paleo-friendly. I have always desired to write ethnic cuisine cookbooks, and you'll find several cultural influences throughout all of my books. But in order to create an entire book based on one specific cultural cuisine, I wanted to have the true experience and understanding of that culture. This was necessary in order to offer you valid and authentic recipes. That is how *Everyday Paleo Around the World* was born. I decided to travel the world and bring back authentic recipes straight from the source. Just deciding to pack up and travel is not all that easy, though. I wanted to include my family in my journeys. That is truly what *Everyday Paleo* is all about—experiencing life to its fullest with the ones you love most.

Once the decision was made to embark on this crazy adventure, my husband and I started formulating a list of places we wanted to go. We began making the arduous plan of how the heck to leave the country for a month without everything in our reality crumbling around us. Of course, friends and family teased us about how rough it must be to have to live abroad for a month. But the reality is that there's a lot of sacrifice, planning, and stress involved in a trip of this magnitude. To top it all off, shutting down my husband's chiropractic business for this length of time was seriously scary. When you operate your own business, there is no such thing as vacation time or sick leave, so it took careful organization, budgeting, and finger crossing to make such a huge undertaking actually work. After weeks of debate, discussion, and logistical decision-making, we decided that our first stop—and, therefore, the first book in this international cookbook series—would be Italy.

We live in a huge world jam-packed with several choices of where to go first, but I thought it would be appropriate to start with a cuisine that everyone loves dearly. As Paleo and gluten-free folks, some of us may feel that Italian food needs to be written off as an indulgence of

the past, especially considering the beloved pizzas and pastas. This book will offer you a true taste of Italy but from a Paleo perspective, and I'm sure you will feel not the least bit deprived after discovering the delicious food that awaits you in the recipe section.

Back to the planning! Along with having to shut down John's business, we also made the decision to homeschool our youngest boys, Jaden and Rowan. We wanted to feel confident that they could leave for a month and not be behind after missing so much school. My oldest son, Coby, however, was a different story. Coby was about to enter his junior year of high school, and homeschooling was simply not an option. Embedded deeply into school activities, extracurricular events, and, of course, his friends, I was in no way going to suggest that Coby depart from traditional schooling with only two years left before college. I was confident, however, that we could arrange something with his teachers so that he could join us on this extremely important trip. After a visit with Coby's high school counselor and emails back and forth with his teachers, he made the difficult decision to stay behind. I was devastated. This was the first big adult decision that my seventeen-year-old son made, and while I begged and pleaded with him (I am way more rebellious than my teenage son), I relented to his calm reply that his junior year in high school was too important to miss. I was now presented with my first epiphany from this journey even though our trip hadn't even really begun. The message was plain as day: Letting go is very, very hard to do.

I'll be honest with you—I still wish Coby had joined us on our adventure because I feel that traveling the world is a better education and experience than school can provide. But that's just my own rebel spirit and not the views or wishes of my very independent and mature son.

We missed you terribly, Coby, but I'm proud of your decision and so lucky to be your mom.

INTRODUCING THE TEAM

So, Italy it was!

There was no way we were going to make this trip possible and accomplish all that we wanted without a team. My intentions were to travel to several regions and to work with as many chefs, farmers, and home cooks as I could squeeze in. I knew that Italy's food varied greatly by region, and I felt it was important to reflect the regional foods in this book as much as possible. I wish I could have lived in Italy for a year and traveled to every region, but that simply wasn't possible. Still, I believe that I've done justice and shown honor to the regions we did explore, and my hope is that my sincerity is reflected in the recipes.

I also wanted to embrace the Italian lifestyle and learn as much as possible from the culture. The history of Italy is so grand that it's almost unimaginable. It was breathtaking to think about what transpired over thousands of years on the very land we were going to walk upon.

As we started to plan our journey, it was clear that I needed help to record all that happened to us on our trip and to capture the memories as they took place. There was no way our little family could do all that we needed to write this kind of book without help. So, I would like to introduce you to the team!

John is my husband, best friend, and literally the glue that holds our family together. Shutting down his thriving chiropractic business was probably the scariest thing we had to do in order to make this trip possible. However, John bit the bullet and jumped in with both feet. John was responsible for just about everything on this trip at one point or another. He held the "boom" (microphone for the video camera) for hours on end without ever tiring, took copious notes, cooked meals for us, remembered everything that I would have forgotten, and made the adventure so much more fun for all of us.

*John
Fragoso*

The "little boys" is how we refer to Jaden and Rowan, being that Coby is the big kid in the family. In reality, they are not all that little anymore, but it's an enduring term that we will most likely use forever. Both boys had birthdays while we were in Italy, and that was the highlight for them. To turn nine and five in an entirely different country than the one they were born in was crazy exciting. Jaden (the nine-year-old) is our foodie, and he was imperative in selecting the recipes that went into this book. Watching him enjoy everything we ate while on our trip was so much fun. Jaden's thoughts and reactions are incredibly genuine, and his comments are always spot-on as he would describe the flavors and aromas that we experienced on our trip. Rowan is an amazing traveler who boarded the plane our baby of only four years old, and came back home a little man of five, proud of his newfound ability to say several Italian words, and asking soon after we returned home when we were going back to Italy! Rowan was born with an adventurous spirit, and his bravery inspires all of us. If Rowan's not afraid, we shouldn't be either, and I continue to learn a lot from my daredevil boy and often try to channel his amazing spirit when I'm faced with uncertainty.

*Jaden
and Rowan
Fragoso*

Damon Meledones

Damon is a highly sought-after photographer and film guru who resides in Silver Springs, Maryland. When he's not doing amazing things like taking photos of the President, shooting Toyota commercials, or filming Beyoncé during her concerts in New York, he also happens to be my awesome cousin who willfully gave up his real life to join us in Italy to capture our trip on camera and video. The truth is, I could never afford him, but Damon is a generous man and family member who agreed to come along to help document our trip. He ended up with way more responsibility than he bargained for, however. Damon is a world traveler and was turned instantly into our go-to guy. Thanks to his experience, Damon's job turned out to be a lot more intense than taking pictures and videos (although that was pretty darn intense also). Damon was our official (whether he liked it or not) travel guide, technology advisor, lead navigator, translator, kid entertainer, comic relief provider, lugging-all-things-that-are-heavy person, and really great hug-giver. Not to mention that he took all the amazing on-location photos that you will find in this book and filmed all the Italian videos on my blog. If you are interested in Damon's photography or film services, you can find him at: www.cameradamon.com

Laura Haren

I have mentioned Laura several times in my previous books and on my blog. Laura is my angel. People come and go in our lives, but when you meet someone you know you will love forever, it's often apparent instantly. Laura is that person to our family. I met her soon after I began coaching at NorCal Strength and Conditioning, where she was one of my first clients in a beginner's class. Laura was also a patient of John's, and John and I both connected with her immediately. Soon after we met, she offered to help us with the boys whenever we needed a break. We took Laura up on her offer, and the rest is history. Immediately, the boys loved her deeply. Now, Laura is like a grandma to them, and she often makes me think of my own mom, how sweet and loving she was with Coby and Jaden, and how much fun she would have had with Rowan. Laura's demeanor and genuine affection for our children is very much like my own mother's, and that means the absolute world to all of us. Although all of my boys call her "Laura," if anyone were to ask, they would refer to her as their grandma. So, it was a no-brainer to decide who would come on our trip to help us with the boys. Laura was amazing and cared for the boys on the days when we had to work late. She also cared for the adults, making sure we were all fed and in bed. She was the mom that everyone needs, and besides that, Laura was quite brave and strong to put up with the Fragoso's for an entire month abroad!

Angela was our last-minute miracle. I had already purchased Coby's plane ticket, optimistic mom that I was. But since Coby decided not to join us, Angela, Laura's daughter, jumped at the chance to be a part of the team! Fresh out of law school and incredibly bright, eager, and organized, Angela's role was crucial. I struggled with last-minute plans and needed guidance to figure out how to get from point A to point B, where to stay in Rome, what side of the island to call our home base when we were in Sardinia, and many other details. Angela stepped in and literally saved the day. She was able to put together the final pieces of our trip and took bounteous notes while in Italy. Angela also kept us on track and contributed more than she possibly knows to the success of this trip. Coincidentally, more than once, we all realized that having a lawyer with us was not a bad idea. Common sense is a must when traveling abroad, and Angela's sharp outlook and amazing savvy made navigating Italy, planning ahead, and staying out of trouble a reality for us all.

Angela
Haren

The remainder of our team members did not make the trip but were equally important to the success of this project.

Mike is our food photographer. More importantly, however, he and his wife, America, and their two little girls, Giana and Catalina, are also our very close friends. Mike took all of the food photos in the recipe section of the book as we worked hard to recreate the amazing dishes that we learned while in Italy. Mike and America spent countless hours on this project, and we are forever grateful for their friendship and dedication. Mike, your photography is brilliant. America, your help is lifesaving, and I'm so happy to have the Lang family as part of the Everyday Paleo Team. Find Mike's amazing photography skills at:
www.jcmichaelphotography.com.

Michael Lang
and Family

Mark Purdy

Mark is my brother and my partner in the kitchen. This is the second book that my brother has worked on with me, and I will not attempt another one without him. Mark is my sous chef extraordinaire, my "idea" guy, and an amazing talent at whatever he sets his mind to. I've had more fun cooking with my big brother than I can express, and I'm so grateful to have Mark as part of my team.

Coby Fragoso

Although Coby did not join us, he is always a key player in the development of my books. Always supportive, interested, loving, and kind, Coby's incredible patience and input literally puts this puzzle together. Coby is my constant companion when writing, and I can't even count the hours we have spent side by side while I write and he studies. He always offers honest advice, criticism, and feedback, and I trust his judgment more than I trust most seasoned adults.

Now you know the crew, so when I mention them throughout our travel log, you'll be able to put faces to the names. Here is a picture of the team that traveled to Italy. We are pictured at the Coliseum in Rome, acting out significant events that took place on our trip. Yes, we were a bunch of silly tourists, but I wouldn't have had it any other way!

Are you ready for takeoff?
Let's go!

ITALY
a brief food history...

Imagine a land full of life, self-sufficient and abundant, with a food culture entirely dependent on one thing: quality ingredients. That is Italy's food perspective in a nutshell. However, our perception of Italian food and its history has been Americanized and is not exactly as we think it is.

What do you imagine when you think about Italian food? Most folks conjure up images of cream or tomato-based sauces atop a pile of pasta or cheese-gooped pizza. Yummy? Yes, but not an entirely accurate representation of truly authentic Italian cuisine. If I were to use the mainstream idea of Italian food as my inspiration to write this book, I could have stayed at home and turned the typical Italian favorites into Paleo and gluten-free fare without ever stepping foot onto Italian soil.

I could not produce a book promising a real Italian experience, however, without first going straight to the source. For example, you will not find a recipe for Fettuccine Alfredo in this book. This dish is not an authentic traditional Italian recipe, but rather one that was created by an Italian chef for his pregnant wife. It was made again for two American movie stars who returned to the States raving about the dish. Because they were well known, word spread quickly. We now see Fettuccine Alfredo in virtually every Italian restaurant in the U.S., but in reality most Italians have never even heard of it! Little details such as this make me feel confident that this book will give you exactly what I hoped it would—a glimpse into the lives and culture of this beautiful and historically rich country, while offering you a chance to cook and enjoy the real food of the Italian people.

The complexity and diversity found in Italy's cuisine varies from region to region. Over the last three thousand years, Italy's food has been influenced by cross-cultural and geographical inspiration. French, Greek, Middle Eastern, Spanish, and German influences are apparent in the foundation of Italian cuisine, and the traditional preparations of specific dishes are set apart based upon location. From north to south and from coast to coast, the inhabitants of each area have made their mark on what is considered to be "Italian" food. However, one common thread is clear: Fresh, local, and quality are the most important aspects of what goes into their food. While the importing of ingredients and the need for food made fast have started to change this amazing food culture, the intimate connection to mealtime and the desire to hold tight to history have kept the real food movement alive and well in Italy, especially in the smaller communities.

For example, the way in which mealtimes are approached dates back to Roman times. Historically, Italians would have a small breakfast, an "important" lunch eaten leisurely and with abundance, and a light, but late dinner. This is more or less the same routine followed in Italy today. We noticed the "late dinner" trend immediately. Most restaurants in Italy do not even open their doors for dinner until 7:00 or 8:00 p.m. Unfortunately, in some areas, the leisurely lunch is starting to dissipate thanks to the influence of modern times and our "hurry up, don't sit to eat, grab a quick bite of processed food, and go back to work" attitudes. The smaller communities tend to stick closer to tradition and have kept the famous Italian approach to mealtime alive and well. This was a philosophy that we enjoyed greatly during our visit.

Interestingly enough, pizza and bread used to be thought of as peasant food. The traditions of both foods remain strong in Italy, however, and bread is served with every meal. The unfortunate truth is that the bread of today's Italy is much different from the bread of ancient Italy. In the past, it was ground by hand between stones and mixed with water, most likely originating from grains that had been fermented or sprouted then dried in the sun. Today, bread in Italy is often made from imported wheat with high-gluten flours. Sometimes, ancient traditions are better left alone, but because of progress, changes such as this are often inevitable.

Today, countrywide, you will find chefs and home cooks using extra virgin olive oil as their main source of fat for cooking, but that has not always been the case. Olive oil is produced mainly in southern Italy, so prior to the ability to ship the oil, the north relied more on butter and animal fats for cooking. Many recipes from the north are still made predominantly with butter, cream, or lard. You will also find less pasta dishes in northern Italy and more meat, corn, and rice dishes.

Southern Italy, however, uses olive oil as their predominant source of fat, and some of the best olive oil in the world is produced there. Most of it isn't exported outside of the country, though. We were privileged to try some of the most amazing extra virgin olive oil I have ever had the pleasure to taste. Unadulterated, handcrafted, from-the-source olive oil is like nothing else in the world and very different from what we find in a typical grocery store. In the recipe section of this book, I give my thoughts on using extra virgin olive oil for cooking, and within the recipes, you'll find my variations and suggestions for using extra virgin olive oil.

The history of Italian cuisine could be an entire book by itself, but this book is about our experiences in the country and, of course, the food. I have separated the sections describing our travels by location, but the recipe section is separated instead by the traditional courses, just like an authentic Italian meal should be served.

MILAN

when nothing else is working, try opening a different door!

Have you ever stepped foot somewhere and felt a magnetic pull as though you were exactly where you were supposed to be? It's the feeling you get when you're house hunting, and you find the house you know is home. Well, that's exactly what I did *not* feel when we stepped out of the airplane and onto Italian soil. After being shepherded through customs and plopped into baggage claim, I instantly felt lost, out of place, confused, and very soon, downright angry. We found our bags and then looked helplessly at our lifeless phones. The plan, organized by Damon, was to pick up an Italian SIM card the following morning so that our phones would work and we could give our numbers out to our Italian contacts. For the time being, however, we were without the comfort of instant connection and communication.

Our flight arrived late in the evening around 9:30 p.m. Italy time, and we were supposed to call the hotel shuttle to pick us up. My cousin, Damon, had arrived a couple of weeks earlier and had been traveling the country with friends. His last email to me suggested that I borrow someone's phone in the airport or use a pay phone to call the hotel shuttle. No problem ... or so I thought. It wasn't nearly that simple. There we were, our little exhausted family in the middle of swirling belts of baggage and a few hundred people shuffling by as they spoke Italian and other languages. If I tried to approach someone, a back would turn toward me or a quick sidestep would make it obvious they didn't want to be bothered. I spotted what looked like a payphone across the nearest baggage belt and left John with the kids to try that option. Making a call was like trying to figure out how to fly a rocket ship. Of course, none of the instructions were in English (why should they be since I was in Italy?), and when I picked up the phone, a recording said something I couldn't comprehend. The pay phone looked like I could use my credit card, but I couldn't figure out how. Of course, I also didn't have a single Euro in my pocket. Wow, this was a poor start!

It was getting later and later, and we had been traveling for almost twenty hours. We were starving and tired, and I suddenly felt very alone and a little bit afraid that I had bitten off way more than I could chew. I travel a lot back home in the States and have always felt

that I could handle anything. But not knowing how to communicate with people and being shunned by folks was defeating to my exhausted body.

I swallowed the lump rising in my throat. As I looked over at my little boys, I could see that they were confident their mommy would figure everything out. I walked over to a customer service counter, and hooray, a man who spoke English greeted me! I pleaded my case and asked him if I could use the phone to call our hotel, and the answer was a flat out "No. We don't let people use our phone. That's why we have pay phones. I can't leave my desk, so I don't know how to help you figure out how to make the phone work." I begged again, but the answer came back in one clearly stated sentence. "I can't leave my station."

I turned around with shaky hands and walked weakly back to my husband and little boys. Trying to be cheerful at this point was just a lame idea, so I told them that I was finished trying, that we had been shot down enough in this place, and suggested we simply go outside to see if we could find someone there to help us. I don't know why we didn't simply leave the baggage claim area to begin with. Maybe the uncertainty of what was outside the doors? Maybe I thought there wouldn't be a payphone in sight or a person to talk to? Maybe I was afraid if we walked through that door, we wouldn't be able to get back in?

When you find yourself in a place where every single solution leads to a dead end, maybe it's a sign to GET THE HECK OUT! As soon as our feet hit the streets of Milan, it was like the clouds lifted. A nice looking older gentleman walked right up to us and asked if he could help us. He spoke very little English, but we understood right away that he was there to help folks just like us who walked out of those doors lost and confused. He led me to a pay phone, gave me two Euros, and showed me how to use the frustrating contraption (actually quite easy to do once you're shown how). As I called the number, he guided John over to another service counter where volunteers could help us further. Someone answered at the hotel, and as soon as I said who I was, they replied with a cheerful, "Ciao, Sarah, your ride has been waiting for you! We have been monitoring your flight and went ahead and sent the van for you."

What a complete turnaround our night had taken. So often, when we're faced with difficult situations, we continue to beat our heads against the proverbial brick wall rather than just

removing ourselves from the situation. I knew immediately that this trip was going to be a life changing one, but just how life changing was yet to be seen.

"Welcome to Italy, boys," I whispered to my husband and little ones as we piled into the van and flew through the winding streets of Milan to our first stop. We tumbled out of the van and into the warm hugs from my cousin, cameraman Damon Meledones, who was waiting for us at The Hotel Ristorante Tre Leoni. The wonderful driver unloaded our things and gave us all hugs and kisses on the cheek. I have never in my life been hugged and kissed by a cab driver, but it was obvious that this type of affection was going to be the norm.

Damon ushered us inside, and we were guided by the hotel owner into their little dining room where a few folks were eating dinner. "Here it goes," I thought, "our first venture through an Italian menu. I hope we survive." How were we going to avoid the pasta? The bread? The gnocchi? The dessert? The gluten-in-everything-everywhere-you-turn country? I knew there was more to Italian food than the typical bread and pasta, but boy, I did not realize just how much more.

We found pages and pages of meat, seafood, grilled vegetables, salads, and fresh fruit along with only a few pages of pasta dishes. Love and warmth swept through me, and we ordered the steak served over arugula with a balsamic reduction, the shrimp cocktail, a mixed grilled meat platter, and some salads. Little Rowan's request for a side of fruit yielded a plate of *real* whole fruit, not even cut. There was an entire apple, a lovely pear, and a bright, beautiful orange. Our amazing journey filled with good food, hope, and love had just begun.

After our bellies were full, the same man who had picked us up from the airport herded us back into his van and drove us down the street to our rooms. It was there that I was faced with my first of many sleepless nights. It took Rowan almost a full week to adjust to the drastic time change, and it was a huge measure of my patience to understand that his little clock would simply take longer to figure out our new routine. Also, he had slept very well on the plane, and I, of course, had not. So, I was ready to be on Italian time while Rowan was ready to play.

*Our first night in Italy had its ups and downs, but
we made it there safe and sound.*

BOLOGNA
there must be a balance

We were only scheduled to stay one night in Milan; the plan was to head to Bologna for my first experience cooking with an Italian chef. Jetlagged and a bit bewildered, we stumbled out the door of our hotel and onto a train toward our destination. The public transportation system is brilliant, even if it is a little confusing at first due to the language barrier. The trains are nice, fairly inexpensive, and go just about everywhere! We all got a kick out of the literal signs that are used as guidance and caution in Italy. One sign looked like a grown man wearing a diaper, hanging from a rope tied to his backpack. We never figured out what this one meant. Other signs were quite obvious, like drawings of people getting smashed between closing train doors.

Fortunately, we all boarded our train without being diapered or smashed by doors, and as we rolled through the countryside, I marveled at the beauty of the land. I still couldn't believe we were on our way to our first cooking destination.

Bologna is in the Emilia-Romagna region of Italy and claims to be the country's culinary capital. It's recognized for its delicious Prosciutto Di Parma, Mortadella, Parmigiano Reggiano, Balsamic Vinegar of Modena, and, of course, the famous regional ragu; Bolognese! When I started doing my research as to where I wanted to visit in Italy, Bologna was first on my list. The entire country of Italy is rich with history, tradition, and culture, but Bologna seemed to be steeped in culinary awesomeness. I didn't want to miss the opportunity to walk the ancient streets and eat the famous Bologna fare.

The house where we stayed was in the countryside of Calderara di Reno about ten kilometers from Bologna. When I inquired about renting the house, the owner informed me that it was only one kilometer from shops and restaurants and right across the street from the train station. So, we decided there was no need to rent a car. The little house we rented was part of a giant old farmhouse that had been renovated into four separate units and rented out to vacationers. The farmhouse was in the countryside and surrounded by orchards and grape fields. Without a car, we literally had to walk the one kilometer (which I

think was actually closer to two), lugging groceries and schlepping the kids. My fear of not being able to exercise while in Italy quickly slipped away.

Everywhere I looked, people were walking. Yes, of course, people drive in Italy, but more often than not, they rely on public transportation or their own two feet. Walking is the most popular mode of transportation in most parts of Italy. The streets are very narrow and difficult to navigate, and fuel is expensive, so, it makes sense to use other means of getting around. As Paleo people, we all know how good it is for us to walk, spend time outdoors, and get plenty of sunshine, and our time in Italy offered daily doses of this healthy prescription.

Our first day in the country house was all about gathering supplies and getting oriented. John and I decided to do the grocery shopping together, and our long hike led us to our first typical Italian grocery store. The produce was bountiful and beautiful, and the selection of meat and seafood was like nothing we had ever seen. I clumsily ordered what I thought was a pound of prosciutto, but what I was given was probably closer to three. We also picked up a whole chicken, some ground beef, and bagged several vegetables. Next, we searched everywhere in the refrigerator section but could not find eggs. It was baffling! I asked someone for the *huevos*, which is Spanish for eggs, until John's brain kicked into gear and remembered that in Italian, eggs are *uovos*. It turns out that in Italian markets, eggs are not kept in the refrigerator but simply on the shelf. This is how we keep our farm fresh eggs at home, but I have never seen eggs in the grocery store fresh enough to keep unrefrigerated! Very cool indeed.

Another tip for shopping in an Italian market is to make sure you weigh and label your vegetables before you try to check out. I had no idea this was a requirement. Most markets are equipped with a scale that prints out labels with prices based on what you purchase. All of the produce has a number associated with it, clearly marked on a handwritten sign. You place your food on the scale, enter the indicated number, and out comes a label with the price. It was pretty embarrassing not to know this. We had to be told by the cashier to go back and start over.

Also, when you leave the market, there is usually one entrance and one exit. Leaving through the entrance rather than the exit will cause a very loud alarm to sound. Yes, we learned this from experience and, to say the least, our first trip to the market in Italy was a little awkward.

The next morning, I was excited and ready for my first cooking lesson in Bologna! John, Damon, and I ran (literally) to catch our train. One of us (who shall not be named) decided to turn down the wrong side street toward the station, and we ended up having to slide down and climb up a six-foot cement canal that was thankfully not full of water. I realized again that staying in shape was not something I would have to worry about. After climbing up and down canals, running through tunnels, and bounding up several flights of stairs, we

reached the platform for our train to the Bologna Cooking School where we would meet my teacher, a native Bolognesi known as Big Carlo. I knew what I wanted to learn, what I wanted to hear, what I wanted to experience, but as with anything new, I had no clue what to really expect.

I had contacted Carlo by email prior to our visit and explained my Paleo objective to him, which was a bit confusing. He did understand my request for gluten-free cooking classes, however. When we left the train station in Bologna, navigated the streets, and found Carlos' sprawling apartment, I felt as if we had been swept back in time. Carlo runs his popular cooking school from his residence, which also doubles as a busy bed and breakfast. His assistant teachers include his sister, Gabriella, who is 82 years old, and his friend, Luciana.

I decided that I loved them all dearly the instant we met. Carlo welcomed us with the traditional hugs and kisses to which we had already grown accustomed. While Damon and John put together the camera equipment, Carlo and I started chatting. We discussed how much had changed over the years since he was a child who watched his mom and grandma cook for his family. Carlo said that cooking used to be a passion for many, but I could tell that he was saddened by the lack of love for quality food that the bustling city's inhabitants had developed. We talked about fast food and how easy it was for his people to acquire "junk" and that the time to create a real meal was no longer necessary thanks to convenience foods. He mentioned how traditionally, pasta and bread were always made by hand. Now, it's easy to buy already prepared food without the labor that used to be involved.

I told him that the same is true in America, and the conversation immediately turned toward food quality, organic growing, and GMO's. Carlo is grateful that his country allows no GMO foods to be grown and that as a whole, Italy still relies very much on local farmers and producers. Unfortunately, this is starting to change as the demand for convenience foods continues to rise, resulting in an increase of processed foods and lack of quality. According to Luciana, most of Italy's wheat is now imported from the United States. In the past, Italy had only two types of flour that were made from locally grown and processed wheat. These were very low-gluten flours that were used to make everything from bread to pastas. Now, they have several options including high-gluten flours for cakes and pastries. As a likely result, the Italian people have seen a frightening rise in Celiac disease and other associated health risks. In fact, many Italians are tested every four years for Celiac, and because of the increase in this disease, gluten-free foods are easy to find almost everywhere in Italy. They even have entire gluten-free markets, and many restaurants offer gluten-free menus. The connection to food quality and an increase in health issues is obvious, and yet, because of convenience and lack of understanding, things only seem to be getting worse rather than better, especially in the larger cities such as Bologna.

According to Carlo, the traditional practices are dying. Carlo admitted that the typical Italian family used to operate with the matriarch of the house in charge of the cooking. It wasn't considered a chore, but an honor. Cooking was a skill passed down from generation to generation that women were passionate about learning. Carlo described the feminist movement as the beginning of the end of the traditional Italian family. I asked Carlo if he thought this was a bad thing, that women were now empowered to work outside the home and to pursue an education with the freedom to decide what they want to do. He agreed that progress is good and that women should choose to do what they wish, but the unfortunate by-product has been a falling off in families eating real food. There has been a serious health decline over the last two decades in Italy, and besides Celiac, there are increases in the cases of Type II Diabetes and heart disease as well.

I could see in Carlo's eyes that he missed how things used to be. For example, lunch used to be a leisurely two hours—a precious, almost coveted time set aside each day to spend with family and friends. Now, the norm in the city is a thirty-minute window to quickly grab some food before heading back to work. I found myself dreaming along with Carlo about how things used to be. Giving up real food and quality time spent with the ones you love are not always the best routes to progress, and I'm faced with the same battles back at home. Even with the knowledge that I have about health and wellness, it's hard to not get caught up in the daily grind and lose sight of what's truly important.

As my thoughts spun in my head, Carlo's next words rang true: "There has to be a balance." Yes, indeed my friend. What a simple, true message. This is something we all say, something

that innately we know, but putting it into practice is another story. Yes, progress is good, but there *must* be that ever-important balance.

We spent two days cooking, laughing, shopping, eating, and drinking amazing wines with Carlo. My favorite part of our time was our visit to the fresh food open-air market in one of the oldest parts of Bologna. Hidden down a narrow street next to the Piazza Del Nettuno is a market that is open every day, and the vendors are all staples of the city's environment and culture. Carlo knows many of the vendors, and he shakes their hands after each transaction, trusting that what they sell him is the best they have. We bought amazing porcini mushrooms, just harvested that morning from the countryside on the outskirts of the bustling city. We also picked up fresh zucchini, spinach, and arugula, as well as calamari that had just been pulled from the sea. I watched a butcher with hands the size of mallets practice his trade. It was a family business, and behind the counter were also his daughter and son-in-law. Carlo looked at me and said, "This man also has the passion. He loves what he does and takes pride in the quality of the meat that he sells." I could see in the butcher's eyes that this was not just his job; it was his life, his duty, his calling. He cared about every person who walked through his door and about every product that left his building. It was such a refreshing experience to see the way in which the vendors conducted their businesses. There is something beautiful about a family-run operation, which includes an attention to detail that no longer exists within large corporations. When a business is your own, passed down from generation to generation, there is more of a desire to please than if it's just a "job."

We also visited a shop that sold the most exquisite cured meats. I ate prosciutto, salami, and the regionally famous mortadella. I thought I had died and gone to heaven. We stopped at Carlo's favorite coffee bar and enjoyed a cappuccino with the local Bologna crowd. We wandered down narrow streets, gazed into windows, and watched happy shoppers enjoy the afternoon. Bologna is an amazing city, filled with joy and wonders around every corner.

Back at Carlo's school, we cooked several amazing dishes together that you will find in this book. Of course, Big Carlo showed me how to make Bolognese just like his mama and grandmother used to. I loved the story he told us about how he used to smell the sauce cooking and would sneak a taste, always burning his tongue because he wasn't patient enough to wait for it to cool. I understand his impatience. This sauce is so good that anyone would have a hard time waiting for it! We also made a calamari and spinach sauce, a zucchini and prosciutto sauce, a delicious butter and tomato sauce called Burro e Oro, garlic sauce, gluten-free gnocchi, tiramisu, and much more.

What an incredible way to start off our trip! It was truly a glimpse of all the good things to come, and I will forever be grateful to Big Carlo, Luciana, and Gabriella for their hospitality, honesty, and genuine desire to share their culture and traditions with us. Most of all, I will carry Carlo's important message with me to always find balance. If you visit Bologna, I highly recommend looking up Carlo and spending at least a day with him at his cooking school. You can find more about Carlo by visiting his website at: wwwBolognaCookingSchool.com.

After cooking with Carlo for two days, we had one day in Bologna as a group where we brought the boys and our whole crew into the city to explore. We wandered the market together and walked over the old cobblestone streets. It felt as if we were in a scene from a movie. Down narrow alleyways, locals sat on the streets and sipped wine, live music played, and little shops and restaurants invited us in at every turn. The little boys were caught up in the excitement, and we were all twisting and tumbling through the magic of Bologna, hand in hand, happy and content. Stopping to rest, John sat with the boys and watched a lively band play on the street while I purchased a bottle of wine. We clinked glasses, laughed, and danced in the streets of Bologna, relishing in our first real taste of this wonderful and laid-back lifestyle. We were swept away by the beauty and mystery of the ancient city and when we left Bologna we were already longing to return.

LE MARCHE

there is always enough time;
in fact, we have all day!

The Marche region is quite possibly Italy's best-kept secret. Located next to the Adriatic Sea with the Emilia-Romagna region to the north, Tuscany and Umbria to the west, and Abruzzo to the south, this part of the world is home to beautiful green hills, an abundance of agriculture, steep sea cliffs, and sandy beaches. The food of Marche is deeply rooted in the peasant tradition, and everyone from the home cook to the executive chef keeps tradition alive so that what you eat is just like mama used to make. The area is also famous for its prized truffles and dry white wines such as the Verdicchio, Bianchello del Metauro, Colli Pesaresi Bianco, Esino Bianco, Colli Maceratesi, Falerio, Offida Pecorino, and Passerina. The wine, the food, the people, and the sheer beauty are Marche trademarks, as well as happiness, peace, and longevity. It is said that in Marche, the native people have the longest life expectancy on earth, and after our visit, I can see why.

Where else in the world are you greeted with kisses from perfect strangers and wrapped warm in the arms of your tour guide? I'm not sure if there is another spot in the universe that has the charm of Italy. Maybe we just got lucky, but the love that welcomed us at every turn was truly a gift. The experience seemed to build upon itself, and as we drove into the little town of Pesaro, we wondered how the trip could possibly get any better. We were scheduled to stay in this region for five days, and we had decided to use the services of a guide for several reasons. First, this area is not as "touristy" as Rome or Tuscany, and the chance of most folks speaking English was pretty slim. Also, we wanted the most authentic farm-to-table experience that we could find, and after doing a bit of research, I was connected with Moreno Moretti, owner and host of Le Marche Holiday (www.lemarcheholiday.net). What Moreno arranged for us was above and beyond my expectations.

Moreno is a young man with a passion to keep his small region alive by supporting local farmers and food suppliers. He is truly an honorable person who has dedicated his career to maintaining the integrity of his culture. Furthermore, Moreno brings his own experience to the table. Moreno grew up on, and still lives on, his family's farm, working hard to help support what is known throughout Italy as the slow food movement. His goal as a tour guide is to not only support Marche's local economy, but to also present visitors with the true experience of Marche. What Moreno offers is the real deal, and he stays true to his word by continuing to support those who grow, serve, and produce food the right way.

Before I share with you the chefs to whom Moreno introduced us, I must first begin our adventure with a story.

We raced down a narrow country road between gorgeous green hills with a giant blue sky looming overhead. I was trying to take it all in while grinding through the gears in our tiny Fiat. "John," I shouted to the backseat, "It's so beautiful! I can't believe it. Are you taking pictures?" I turned my head quickly to my passenger and guide, Moreno, and asked frantically, "Moreno, should you call ahead to the truffle hunter and to the chef because we're going to be late, and I need to stop for gas. And we should get our coffee to go!" The kids were smashed in the back with John, and both of them were laughing and leaning into each other around every sharp curve. But despite the view and their cute giggles, I was all business and in a hurry, not wanting to insult the truffle hunter or the award-winning chef who were awaiting our arrival. Without any caffeine in my system, I was also navigating through winding narrow roads in a tiny car running low on gas. I tore into a roadside fuel station and asked John to get us espressos to go. "Hurry," I hollered at him. "While you run in, I'll figure out the gas!"

I then remembered our quiet guide, Moreno, and apologized to him for our tardiness. Before Moreno could reply, John ran back from the store and handed us our espressos. "How am I supposed to shift this darn car while I drink my coffee?" I asked breathlessly as the fuel attendant stared at my antics like I was from outer space. I lurched the car out of the station like the silly tourist I was.

Finally, Moreno had a chance to speak. "Sarah," he said calmly in his lovely Italian accent, "why are we in such a hurry? We have all the time in the world, my friend. We have all day!" We laughed as Moreno struggled to drink his coffee while I drove like a mad woman, and he admitted this was his first time drinking a coffee "to go." He wondered how Americans could enjoy their days without stopping to enjoy an espresso. Everywhere in Italy, there are coffee bars, even at the gas stations. What a healthy habit to stop for a few minutes to have your coffee and connect with other people. Why do we not allow the extra ten minutes to nurture ourselves with a much-needed breather?

Moreno was so right—because of the hustle and bustle that is normal in my world, I lost sight of this simple perspective. Instead of constantly being in a hurry, I needed to realize that there is always plenty of time to get where I am going or do what needs to be done. In fact, we noticed that time did move slower while we were in Italy because we stopped asking it to hurry up. We just lived and fit in what we could, knowing that there was always tomorrow. Our family had to conform to the Italian pace of life; no one would let us speed them up to our pace. So, instead, we slowed down to theirs. This resulted in a splendid discovery. We were still productive, we still worked hard, we still kept our focus, but we also took time to enjoy our lives.

Moreno introduced us to more than amazing chefs and fabulous food. He also introduced us to the reality that we are living way too quickly, and killing ourselves in the process. He opened our eyes to how humbly life should be lived. I will never forget when he told us, "Italians, compared to Americans, we are lazy, yes, but we still get it all done. We are hard workers, but we know how to rest and live and eat!" It really is that simple, but we Americans are so wrapped up in cramming in as much as possible. If we think about this viewpoint from an evolutionary perspective, it's all quite obvious. Our ancestors had no concept of needing to hurry up. They hunted for food and rested to preserve their energy for the next time they needed to move quickly. They played and spent time with their families. Progress is good in many ways, but it has messed up this simplistic formula. Now, each morning when I wake up, I try to remind myself to be a little bit more like Moreno and to slow down because the reality is; we have all day.

One of our first adventures with Moreno was a truffle hunt in the beautiful countryside of Ascoli Piceno. The boys laughed as we imagined rebellious and elusive truffles while our car wound through a maze of green, misty hills toward our destination. We came to a halt outside a gate filled with signs, all in Italian, but the message came through loud and clear: guns, knives, and bigger guns awaited us if we entered without warning. "Wow," I thought, "maybe this day is going to be more suspenseful than I imagined." Moreno directed us to the "other" gate that was marked in a friendlier fashion with only one giant padlock and no scary signs. The huge yard was filled with the cuddliest, cutest, barking dogs I have ever seen. Despite the foreboding warning on our initial approach, when the truffle hunter emerged from his house romantically nestled in the quiet of Marche's bliss, you could see his gentle spirit behind his blue eyes and his love for his dogs.

Giorgio is a third generation truffle hunter specializing in finding the treasured white truffle or *tartufi bianco*. He has made his livelihood by perfecting the art of finding these amazing little buried gems. For the last four generations, the family has lived in the same home and hunted the nearby hills that are public property, yet rarely visited due to the remote location. Those who do visit the surrounding hills are truffle hunters like Giorgio, all looking for the prized tartufi bianco nestled mystically in the ground under looming oaks and near small streams.

Giorgio picked out two of his dogs, and our hunt was about to begin. It will forever be ingrained in our memories as a wonderful experience. The Italian people are passionate about everything they do, and I felt like Giorgio and his daughter were on their first hunt ever. The dogs were bounding and leaping, sniffing and snorting. Almost right away, we were close to finding one! Giorgio handed Moreno a scoop of fresh dirt, and Moreno buried his nose into the pungent soil. Warm and sumptuous, deep and satisfying earthy smells filled the air as the dogs flung the soil wildly in search of the prize.

We found several truffles that day, and Giorgio said we were good luck. On the contrary, I think they brought us the good luck by offering us the opportunity to join them as they demonstrated their family's trade. The care that Giorgio took of his dogs, the love they have for their land and for preserving its beauty, and the obvious connection they have as a family is astonishing. Giorgio and his daughter were happy to have our boys pet their dogs and marvel at the truffles, which are literally prized possessions and the source of income that feeds their family. They were happy to share their art with complete strangers and proud as they should be of the simple and beautiful life they live. Our family was enamored with this way of life and eager to apply it to our own lives: Live simply. Tread softly. Love deeply. Eat well.

We left the truffle hunt refreshed and alive with the dirt still on our shoes and the earthy smell in our nostrils. I was scheduled to meet and cook with Chef Samuele Ferri, owner of Osteria Del Parco situated in the little village of Acqualagna, which is home to the annual National Truffle Festival. This village is an often overlooked, yet a beautiful and charming part of Italy.

Before our time together in Samuele's kitchen, we were treated to lunch, which was an unforgettable culinary experience. We had endless antipasti of thinly sliced carpaccio, fresh arugula, tomatoes, shaved truffles, delectable prosciutto, aged balsamic vinegar, and fragrant local wines. From the very beginning of our meal to the end, I knew that setting foot in Samuele's kitchen would be a huge honor that I would not take for granted. Samuele is considered a master chef of French and Italian cuisine and started cooking at age fourteen. Now, twenty-four years later, he is still as carefree as a teenager, but a true artist in his kitchen. The two recipes inspired by Samuele that you will find in this book are the Lamb with Aromatic Herbs (page 208) and the Sweet Potato Soufflé (page 126). When you find yourself in Acqualagna, please visit my friend, Samuele, and be sure to ask for anything with truffles!

The next day, Moreno took us straight to a little slice of heaven. I thought nothing could top the beautiful countryside of the truffle hunt, but I was wrong. We were scheduled to cook with Chef Virginio Baldelli at his family-owned and operated osteria, Antica Osteria Da Gustin. The osteria is situated in the tiny village of Serrungarina, population twelve. Yes,

ITALIAN
CUISINE

only twelve people live in the tiny village, which is reminiscent of some sort of wonderland that I thought only existed in dreams. Travelers and folks from neighboring villages come to visit Chef Virginio and taste his food, olive oils, and wines.

Virginio used to be a highly respected sommelier/manager in Pittsburgh, Pennsylvania, but after a few years of living the madness of the American way, he and his wife decided to move back to the little village in Italy and reopen the osteria originally operated by his grandfather. Using the same principles and techniques as his grandfather, and relying solely on locally grown and produced food, Chef Virginio has kept tradition alive and is a true example of the slow food movement. When Virginio and his family are not working at the osteria, they travel around the Marche region, meeting new farmers and producers. They support these farmers and producers by offering their goods at the osteria. Everything is made by hand and presented with love, and the tiny osteria proves that attention and quality matter most. With only five tables, you truly experience dining in the atmosphere of home. The view alone from the porch of Osteria Da Gustin is worth the plane ride across the Atlantic, and if I ever have the opportunity to visit Italy again, you can bet I will spend time in the peace and serenity of the little village of Serrungarina.

Oh, and the glorious food! Chef Virginio's huge hands created the most delicate dishes, fresh and simple but so amazingly succulent. Earthy mushrooms harvested just that morning, chicken that was not "just chicken" but meat so tender and flavorful that we were silent as we ate. Fish cooked the traditional way with no reason to change what has been tried and true for generations. Italian roasted potatoes with fresh herbs and local, fragrant, taste bud-enticing extra virgin olive oil.

I love that Virginio gave up his highly respected job in the States to come home and keep his family traditions alive. His gift to the tiny village has breathed life back into what could have become a crumbling ghost town. The osteria, perched on a hill in the seventeenth century building, holds up strong to the weathering of time, and Virignio and his family are true heroes of real food. Sometimes, the most important decisions have everything to do with focusing on family, tradition, food, and savoring the smaller accomplishments in life that lead to greater rewards in the long run.

My favorite memory of Osteria Da Gustin involves watching Virginio and his wife's attention to their patrons. A young family came in for dinner with their little boy who was probably only three. He toddled up to the counter and waited patiently for Virginio's wife to hand him a fresh slice of prosciutto. Every time, she leaned forward and brushed his check lightly with her fingers or kissed his forehead. It was so beautiful. Remembering the simplicity of it all and the warmth, comfort, and love that surrounded us during our time spent at this magical place brings tears to my eyes.

The recipes that you will find inspired by Chef Virginio include the Herbed Chicken with Pancetta, page 238, the Baked Fish and Sweet Potatoes, page 228, the Mushroom Antipasto, page 90, and the Italian Roasted Sweet Potatoes, page 128.

ABRUZZO
even when it's bad, it can still be the best day ever!

I thought long and hard about leaving this portion of our trip out of the book entirely, but the story of the fateful two days of our agriturismo or "farm stay" must be told. I will not say exactly where we stayed, as my purpose is to maintain the integrity of our hosts. Our different worldviews are not a reflection of character and we all have our own ways that should be honored; despite opinions or perceptions.

Everything was going well until we ended up at what was the most highly anticipated part of our adventure. We scheduled a farm stay near Abruzzo in central Italy about two hours south of Rome. As we drove from Marche to our new destination, the beauty that loomed in front of us blew us all away. As the elevation rose, unbelievably majestic mountains appeared in front of us. They were beyond what I could ever have imagined. I almost cried because of the sheer beauty. Our kids were all "wows" and "oohs" and "aahs" as we drove through the kilometers of tunnels. We emerged from each one to find another breathtaking scene of mountaintops jutting through expansive puffs of clouds, lush, green hillsides, and old villages hanging off of sheer cliffs. It was like we were driving through the Swiss Alps mixed with the tropics, a side of Italy and a big dose of some magical land created by Disney. We kept calling Damon, Angela, and Laura in the car ahead of us, saying, "Can you believe this view?"

It all started like a fairytale, but as we climbed higher into the mountains, the warm and mild climate of the Marche region faded away. Soon a cold rain was hammering down upon us. We were unfazed, though, because we're all tough and weathered. We were fine with the elements and happy to be on our way to a new adventure.

My boys were excited because both of them were going to have birthdays during our time at the farm. Rowan would turn five, and three days later, Jaden would turn nine. We reminded Rowan that he would celebrate his birthday on a real farm in Italy! Well, best laid plans, as they say...

We arrived at the farm well past 8:00 p.m. It was dark and cold, and while it was hard to see exactly where we were, it did not look like a farm at all. When we stepped out of our cars, it smelled like a farm, but the buildings around us, though quaint and charming like old Italy should be, did not appear as if abundant fields, horse stables, or livestock surrounded them. I was excited for the farm stay because the owners were entirely self-sustainable, eating only what they could grow or raise on their farmland.

The farmer's son greeted us warmly as we all clambered out into the rain, and he hustled us into the main room where dinner was waiting for us. Hungry and tired from our travels, we all sat around the table. Plates of tomatoes arrived, followed by some sort of summer squash and a large salad. Finally, a small plate of what we were told was pork arrived. The vegetables were not very flavorful, but at least they were fresh. The meat was a bit tough, but we were happy to have food to fill our bellies.

As we ate, the farmer's son informed me that my first cooking lesson would be the next day. He said I could also participate in the killing of the rabbit that would be the main ingredient of my cooking lesson. The next day was Rowan's birthday, and I wasn't sure I wanted to commemorate it by killing a rabbit. But I swallowed hard and thought about the prospect presented to me. Here I was way out in the middle of nowhere on a farm in Italy where they are self-sustained. If they want to eat animals, they have to kill them, something I understand and have total respect for. Still, rabbits are warm and fuzzy, and I don't really like the way they taste. So, having to slaughter one as part of the bargain did not sound like my cup of Paleo tea. I let the farmer's son know that I would witness the process but would not participate in carrying out the act.

After dinner, we were led to our rooms. They were humble, which was fine because we weren't expecting or wanting luxury. The beds were cots covered with old blankets, and each room had a bathroom with a shower. It was cold and damp, and the farmer's son informed us that the heaters in the rooms were set to go off only once early in the morning and once late in the evening. We bundled up for the night, and as it grew colder, we shoved the boys between us to keep them warm. It was pretty darn miserable, but we slept since we were exhausted from our long day of travel.

The next morning, Jaden and Laura both woke feeling ill with fever, chills, body aches, and stuffy noses. Jaden is as tough as nails and rarely gets sick, but he felt bad enough to stay in bed. Despite the situation, Rowan was cheerful and excited for his birthday events, but the rain continued to pour down with gusto. The farmer's son came to get John, Damon, and I because it was time to slaughter the rabbit. In the meantime, Laura pulled herself together and asked if she could use the kitchen to make a cake for Rowan—we had found a gluten-free cake mix at a store in Pesaro before we left the Marche region. Jaden was tucked in bed, Rowan was in the kitchen with Laura, and the rest of us walked down a few steps to the barn.

From the ceiling hung ropes and chains, and two giant barrels sat nearby. Damon readied his camera, and the old farmer pulled a big black rabbit from the barrel. In my opinion, what we witnessed next was inhumane. There was no respect for this poor animal, and the slaughtering appeared to be ritualistic and without concern for how much the animal suffered. Since this experience I have researched how rabbits are typically slaughtered, and what we watched play out on the farm in Abruzzo was not anything close to how it's typically done. I will spare you the gory details, but I will say that I was immediately traumatized. I left the scene confused, crying, and distraught. John didn't speak. My strong and always courageous husband had tears in his eyes and we both immediately wanted to leave. As we walked away from the scene, I tried to rationalize what we had witnessed. I did not want to offend these seemingly nice people who genuinely appeared to want to share their lives, culture, and traditions with us. They had been living their lives here for generations, and this was obviously how things were done, but I wasn't sure if I could stomach anymore. I huddled together with John, and we decided to keep moving forward. Somewhere in all of this, there had to be a lesson.

Back in the warmth of the kitchen (the only warm place we could find on the farm), the farmer's wife showed me how they prepared the rabbit. As the meat boiled, she made a soup that was the one food takeaway from this leg of our journey. It was fairly humble, but I will say proudly that my rendition of the Carrot and Fennel Soup (page 154) is one of my favorite recipes in this book.

Later that evening, Laura and Jaden both looked worse than they had in the morning, unable to eat a single thing. My sweet Rowan, oblivious to all that was happening around him, happily ate a big helping of food. We then sang "Happy Birthday" to him and passed around his gluten-free cake. It was dry and not very tasty, but the beauty in all of this was Rowan's amazing spirit. He did not have a typical birthday party, was stuck inside all day because of the torrential rain, had been served inedible rabbit and bland soup for his birthday dinner, and finished it off with a dry, tasteless gluten-free cake. Still, after his birthday song, he climbed into my lap and announced, "Mom, this is the best birthday ever!" We all laughed, and I cried a little because despite feeling uncomfortable in that place, I realized how much we are blessed. Even when all around us is dark and a little uncertain, I'm reminded of the love my family shares and that as long as we are all together, everything will be okay. This moment, this poignant life lesson, was obviously the reason for our journey to this farm.

Needless to say, we cut our stay short. After another cold and miserable night, we collected ourselves and drove to the neighboring village. We found a warm restaurant and ordered steaks and salad. We all ate more in one sitting than we had in those two days at the farm. Laura and Jaden perked up almost immediately from the warmth and real food. We headed back to the farm with new resolve, and I bravely let the farmer's son know that we would be leaving three days earlier than planned. We gathered our belongings and headed for Rome.

We had no idea where we were going to stay once in Rome, but it didn't matter. Adventure was a huge part of this trip, and anywhere would be better than the place we were leaving. Resourceful as always, Angela found us a great apartment to rent near the Trevi Fountain for three days until our flight to the island of Sardinia.

Looking back, I'm grateful for the experience at the farm because of the memories I have of Rowan's "best birthday ever." My baby turned five in the middle of what felt like hell to us, but it wasn't hell to him because he *wanted* to be happy. If I'm ever having a bad day, I'll reflect back to our time on the farm because, ultimately, it's up to me to turn things around, change my perspective, and make it the best day ever.

ROME
a sweet sanctuary

*R*ome was a sweet sanctuary, with a few caveats. Driving through the city was a nightmare that made me appreciate all of our clearly marked rules and regulations back in the States. The city itself, however, was an oasis of warmth and comfort after our time in Abruzzo. While trying to find the apartment that Angela had found, we ended up getting lost. I followed Damon through the winding, crazy streets, trying to remember to breathe and not blink so as not to miss a car shooting out of nowhere, a sudden turn, an unmarked street, or a wildly running pedestrian. I think we would have been lost on the streets of Rome forever if it weren't for Tony, the gentlemen from whom we were renting our apartment. He guided us by cell phone down the narrow alleyways that were hardly wide enough for our tiny Fiats. Finally, Tony emerged magically on a dark street corner, like an angel in a helmet on a motor scooter, and he led us the last couple of blocks to our destination.

A hot shower and warm bed was more attractive at the moment than the bustling streets outside the apartment, but Tony greeted us with some unexpected news. We had planned on taking the three short days we had in Rome to rest and recover, but Tony informed us that he had a friend who was a highly respected home chef who offered cooking lessons to tourists that visited the city. Even better? She was Celiac and understood our need to eat gluten-free. She offered to create a meal for us, as close to Paleo as possible. I had to say yes to that, exhausted or not. It was as if I was meant to work with Tony's friend.

Our meeting was scheduled for the following evening, and Tony informed me that she planned to show me how to make the most amazing and authentic Ossobuco, Risotto Milanese, Pesto, and Tortino De Zucchine we had ever tasted. PERFECTO! Also promised was the opportunity to sample the special extra virgin olive oil that she purchased from a close friend from southern Italy who bottled his prized possession from his own ancient olive grove. I was suddenly rejuvenated and grateful for our decision to come to Rome!

The next day, we ventured out to explore the ancient city. Our little apartment was situated only a few blocks from the Trevi Fountain. As we strolled along the busy streets, chatting and peering into shops, the scene reminded me of any other big, bustling city until we turned a

corner. Looming above us was an ancient reminder that the streets we were treading upon held more history than my brain could comprehend. The beauty of the Trevi Fountain took my breath away. I couldn't even begin to imagine the work involved in creating such a masterpiece, and yet, they somehow built it without modern equipment. The stories from that ancient era unraveled before our eyes, engraved in travertine and marble. This was my first glimpse of the power that is Rome. The emotion that stirred within me is truly without description, as images of the millions of people who had been there before, loved there before, died there before, and lived their lives there before was intensely real and powerful.

They say that those who throw a coin into the fountain are sure to return to Rome. So, yes, of course, we all tossed in coins, and it goes without saying that we all want to return to this enchanted city. We were also making a donation. An estimated 3,000 Euros are thrown daily into the fountain, and the city uses the money to subsidize a supermarket for the needy. I could have stayed by the fountain all day, but my cooking lesson was about to begin. So, we went back to the apartment to greet our guests of honor while we were still tingling with the excitement that is cultivated by simply being in Rome.

The two beautiful women who walked through our doors to cook with us were full of charm and light, and we were greeted with the expected hugs and kisses. They introduced themselves as Anna Maria Cuzzocrea and Anna Romeo. Anna Maria was the head chef (and the one with Celiac) and Anna was her close friend and assistant. Both ladies wore dresses and boots and professional matching aprons and hats. They were pros, ready to show us their culinary prowess. I was extremely interested to hear about how Anna Maria's diagnosis had affected her life as a chef who is serious about Italian traditions. As they set up shop, we chatted, and Anna Maria opened up about her history.

As long as Anna Maria could remember, she had not felt well. She suffered from what sounded like irritable bowel syndrome, and she grew sicker as the years went on. She was finally diagnosed with Celiac in the early 2000s but did not want to admit that she could no longer eat or cook several food items that she loved. Finally, after living in extreme discomfort for years, she decided to go gluten-free and immediately began to improve. Today, Anna Maria continues to teach tourists how to cook authentic Italian cuisine, but she doesn't eat anything containing gluten. Her story is not unique and confirmed that gluten intolerance is becoming more and more prevalent in Italy. It was also nice to connect with someone else who understood how we ate.

Then, it was time to cook! We were mesmerized as we watched Anna Maria and Anna prepare an amazing meal of truly authentic Italian dishes. They focused on rustic and traditional dishes seasoned with fresh herbs and high quality extra virgin olive oil. We felt spoiled, eating like kings and queens in our lovely apartment in the beautiful city of Rome.

The next day was Jaden's birthday, and his request was to visit the Vatican, especially the Sistine Chapel. What a way to spend Jaden's ninth birthday! As we wandered the halls of

the Vatican that eventually led to the Sistine Chapel, I couldn't believe I was actually there. I also couldn't believe that my nine-year-old felt compelled to visit the most impressive church in existence as a way to celebrate his birthday. We were all moved by the images, art, and history that surrounded us. We were literally standing in the history books. We walked the halls that had been walked by Michelangelo and looked up at the images he painted with his own hand. It was mesmerizing, beautiful, and amazing. The boys were both now a year older and we all had grown and learned more together in the last few days than I could have possibly imagined. I'm glad we were able to experience it all together as a family. Leaving Rome was going to be hard, but our last adventure awaited us.

SARDINIA
life long friendship
and kindness for kindness' sake

We often hear about folks performing random acts of kindness or being helpful without asking for anything in return. In reality, however, how often do we meet people with no hidden agenda? Well, we experienced someone like that in Marcello Sechi, a gentleman who had been notified from my Facebook post that we were coming to Italy and offered to help us on our quest. Marcello's sister, who lives in the States, is an *Everyday Paleo* blog reader who also has my books and had regained her health thanks to Paleo. This was all the reason Marcello needed to offer his support and guidance. Because of his sister's newfound health, he wanted to pay it forward. Without the connection I had made with Marcello, we might not have even ventured to the island of Sardinia. I am a firm believer that everything happens for a reason, but only if you are open to opportunities when they present themselves. Our visit with Marcello only further solidified this belief for me.

We arrived on the island late at night after a fiasco at the airport in Rome. We soon realized that not too many parties of eight with tons of luggage arrive on Sardinia on little commuter flights. Nearly ten million Euros worth of charges later for bags that were over the weight limit, we arrived on the island a bit frustrated by our oversight, but excited. We had rented a little house near the beach (which isn't hard to do since we were, after all, on an island). The rental agent was kind enough to meet us at the airport, and we followed her through dark, winding roads to our destination.

After Rome, it was awesome to breathe in fresh sea air and listen to the crashing waves from our back porch. I had a feeling of calm in my soul. Once again, I felt like we had found our second home. Italy is a place that holds many magical locations, and the Italian way is contagious. Once we arrived at our destination, the little boys were leaping and bounding through the beach house, ecstatic that they would be able to put their feet in the Mediterranean Sea the next day when only a couple of weeks ago they were wading in the Adriatic. Before we crawled into the welcoming beds, we realized that the house had shutters on all of the windows that blocked out every speck of light, even from the full moon. Our sleep that first night on Sardinia was deeper and more peaceful than any night we had yet spent in Italy. It was a sign of what was to come, and as it always seems to be, the best is typically saved for last.

The next day, we would experience another epic adventure filled with total acceptance, tranquility, warmth, amazing food, and love from the people of Sardinia. In the morning, Damon, Angela, John, and I hugged Laura and the little boys goodbye and drove into the town of Cagliari to meet Marcello. He was kind, eager, and genuinely happy to meet us and even more excited to show us his island. Marcello's passions include food and culture, but family comes first for him. He's a loyal husband, father, brother, and son. It was clear where he focuses his priorities, which is noble and honorable in my opinion.

I had been able to speak to Marcello via Skype prior to our arrival, and he had promised an authentic Sardinian experience. He had been a culinary student, studying under Michelin Star Chef Roberto Petza. During his time as Chef Roberto's student, he connected with several other well-known chefs on the island. Before we began our culinary tour, however, Marcello took us on a quick tour of Cagliari and gave us a brief history lesson of his island home.

Sardinia is situated smack in the middle of the Mediterranean Sea and, for centuries, was a desired acquisition by many neighboring countries. The Spanish, the French, and the Romans have all at some point ruled Sardinia, and the original city walls still cradle cannonballs from battles long ago. One interesting fact unbeknownst to me until our visit was that the Sardinian people speak different dialects, depending on their location and which country had more influence in the area. The island belongs to Italy, but the people there consider themselves "Sardinians." Of course, the influences of different countries are also found in the food.

Marcello's contacts were priceless. He had spoken to several people who were more than willing to work with us and share their skills and secrets. Our first visit was right in the town of Cagliari at Vineria Ristorante Eno with Chef Davide Piras and owner Stefano Lai. When you first walk into Eno, a majestic bar that includes a small area to hang out, relax, and have a drink before dinner greets you. Downstairs is the intimate, warm, and cozy dining area that's not too big and not too small. It feels like a five-star restaurant that's wrapped in the warmth and comfort of someone's gracious home. Situated only a few blocks from the sea, Eno serves typical Sardinia fare with a variety of seafood, meats, and some pastas. It wasn't typical in taste for us, though. It was beyond amazing! Eno is a popular hangout for locals and tourists, and I'll travel to Sardinia again just for Davide's food.

What also draws customers to Eno is the obvious care, love, and passion of everyone who works there. These people are professionals from head to toe. Chef Davide is young, handsome, and confident in the kitchen. He spoke to me in Italian, which was awesome. I didn't intimidate him at all, and he understood right away that food was the language we had in common. I hardly needed translating from Marcello after four weeks in the country.

Much like the previous chefs had expressed, the lesson from Chef Davide was clear that you must use quality ingredients. Everything must be fresh and in season, and you must know precisely where your food comes from. I did not see a single canned or frozen item in the pristine kitchen.

Davide and his brigade showed us how to make a basic tomato sauce that is now a staple in our house and a recipe that you'll find in this book. Davide also created stuffed zucchini flowers, a fish burger served with simple but delicious coleslaw, marinated sardines, the most elegant and delicate eggplant Parmesan, pumpkin cream with prawns, and a mussel and clam soup. My own renditions of most of these amazing dishes can be found in the recipe section.

After each recipe, Davide would look at me and say in English, "This one will be front page in your book, no?" His confidence was wonderful. After our time spent in the kitchen, we stayed and ate dinner. I sat with John, Damon, and Angela outside on the patio and savored delicately grilled octopus, a delicious Chopped Chicken Salad (page 86), Steak with Savory Onions and Grapes (page 220), a potato soufflé with creamy pesto sauce, and much more. Eating Paleo, or at least pretty darn close to it, was not challenging at this restaurant. Maybe it was the wine, but we all wanted to stay in Sardinia and discussed among ourselves if we should bring Coby over on the next plane and never go home.

There is so much good in this world, but it's easy to lose sight of it with all the destructive news headlines. I really did want to stay in Sardinia forever, away from "reality." As I lay in bed that night, though, I contemplated whether what we were experiencing was reality and whether our lives back home were just a lie. Maybe all I needed was to adopt the same philosophies back home to recreate the wonderful sensations of a life that's a bit fuller and moves a bit slower.

Day two on Sardinia, Marcello directed us to the restaurant owned by his mentor and Michelin Star Chef Roberto Petza. I'll be honest. I was feeling some wonderment at the prospects of meeting the man. The way Marcello described Roberto, I could tell this was going to be a chef who ruled his kitchen, and rightfully so. Who was I to walk in and disrupt his routine, his success, and his passion? I was just a girl, a stranger from America asking him to please not serve me his bread and teach me how to make his award-winning fare. I don't typically play the nervous game, though, so I walked confidently into Roberto's kitchen and shook the hand of the man who turned simple ingredients into culinary magic. His entire staff was standing at attention, the kitchen gleamed, pots of boiling deliciousness sat atop one of his two six-burner stoves, and a giant fish pulled only hours ago from the Mediterranean glared at me with empty eyes on the pristine stainless steel counters.

I watched Chef Roberto break down the giant fish with the precision of a ninja, and I wished I could channel his butchering skills that only come from years of experience. As he worked, he explained his point of view. He tries to grow as much of his own food as possible. What he does not grow, he sources from local farmers and producers. He showed me a picture on his phone of the lamb he had just purchased to be slaughtered and butchered for his restaurant. The photo was taken when he personally went to the farm to pick out the lamb he wanted. Just that morning, he went to the fish market to purchase the giant fish that would be the staple ingredient for his menu that evening. Speaking of his menu, it constantly changes based on the season and ingredients that Roberto can find that meet with his approval.

Watching Roberto cook was like watching a beautiful waltz. I could see his connection with, and the respect he had for, the food he prepared, and what he created was not based on recipes but on intuition and passion for what he does.

I truly believe that food tastes better when made with love, but Roberto puts more than love into his food. It's a fusion of knowledge, understanding, and an infinite connection to his culture, as well as the belief that we should know where our food comes from. There was nothing processed or convenient in his kitchen. Everything was made from scratch, by hand, and while they did take advantage of some modern appliances and techniques, Roberto loves to slow cook and marinate. I would call his food a synthesis of flavors, and thanks to his world travels, I even found some Asian influence in his preparations. Roberto's culinary point of view is to pay close attention to pairing sweet with savory, making sure the textures complement each other. He also makes certain that each and every dish he serves has stunning visual appeal. Watching Roberto plate his food is like being witness to art in motion.

During our time together, I observed Roberto make the fresh fish he had just butchered into several tantalizing dishes. He followed up the seafood preparation with a delicately prepared and to-die-for pork belly. Finally, he made two delectable gluten-free desserts. What you'll find influenced by Roberto in this book include the Fish Soup (page 148), Pork Belly with Pomegranate Reduction (page 218), Fish with Potato Cream (page 230), and the Poached Pears (page 252).

After cooking with Roberto, he invited us to tour his restaurant and stay for dinner. We visited his wine and cheese cellar and ate a meal fit for kings and queens. Roberto's innovative cuisine was truly an experience I will never forget. If you ever venture to the island of Sardinia, you must visit the little town of Siddi and the restaurant S'Apposento a Casa Puddu and say hello to Roberto for me. You will not regret it.

The next day, we drove to the east side of Sardinia to a coastal town called Arbatax that relies heavily on tourism to keep its economy alive and well. The restaurant, Lucitta, is only open seasonally. Peak vacation season had just ended a couple of weeks prior to our visit, and the restaurant was currently closed for the winter. Although this should have been the owner's time for vacation and relaxation with her family, the wonderful Chef Clelia and her husband opened their doors just for us. Clelia has been a chef for only five years; she trained under Chef Roberto, who is the go-to man on the island for aspiring chefs wanting to fine-tune their skills. I was curious if we would receive a similar demonstration at Lucitta since Clelia had trained with Roberto, but I was happily surprised to find that Clelia has her own cutting-edge approach to her Italian culinary roots.

Seafood was her specialty, and with the Mediterranean literally steps from the front door of the restaurant, I could see why. Clelia's style is modern eclectic cuisine crashing head on

with typical dishes of Sardinia. When Clelia is not operating and cooking at her successful restaurant, she and her husband help run their family's farm. Their income is subsidized based on profits from what the farm produces year-round. The other benefit of being part of the family farming operation is that all of the produce served at Lucitta comes right from Clelia's own backyard. It was so wonderful to find this trend in Italy of cooking and selling what you can grow yourself, or at least knowing exactly where the food you are offering comes from. It's such a beautiful and simple idea that goes hand in hand with living a Paleo lifestyle.

Clelia's smile is contagious, as is her warm and good-natured approach to cooking. The first word that comes to mind when describing the cuisine we cooked together is "fresh."

Clelia used simple ingredients, all in season, to create innovative and surprising dishes. Her plating skills are genius, and I loved watching her attention to even the smallest details. Again, dear readers, it's passion for real food and care in the little things that make Italian cuisine so special. I'm grateful for the validation of the importance of these small elements as the stuff that truly matters. Understanding the work it takes, the care involved, and the quality of our food should not be something we only wish for; it should be the standard.

Although Clelia spoke very little English, by this point in our trip, I could understand most of the Italian words related to food and needed just a tiny bit of help from Marcello to translate her instructions. Marcello did help relay Clelia's story about how she came to be the highly renowned chef she is today in five short years. After opening a pizzeria with partners that did not work out, Clelia branched out on her own and started creating her spin on traditional Sardinian fare. Today, Lucitta is swarming with tourists during the busy

season as a result of Clelia following her passion. The recipes in this book that are based on Clelia's dishes include the Shrimp with Fennel Cream (page 234), Stuffed Calamari or Chicken (page 236), Red Bell Pepper Sauce (page 166), and the Fish with Celery Cream (page 226). Please visit Lucitta if you are in Sardinia, and give Clelia a hug from me.

Our last day of cooking on Sardinia was inland on a farm stay, or agriturismo. Marcello assured us that we would have an amazing day and that the chef was professional, talented, and someone we simply had to meet. We were headed to Agriturismo Casa Marmida to work with Chef Andrea Pani.

Chef Andrea's family owned and operated the farm, and Andrea was in charge of just about everything. He cooked all of the meals for their visitors, helped care for, slaughter, and butcher the animals, tended the fields, and cared for the maintenance of the farm in general. Casa Marmida was nestled among lush fields in the middle of the island. When we drove down the long driveway, I could tell immediately that this was going to be a unique and exciting experience. Gleaming little buildings (obviously the guest's quarters) awaited us, and to the left of the guest rooms was the common area where visitors gathered for meals. Walking into the dining area was like walking back in time. The building was extremely old but had been beautifully renovated with inviting and warm décor. Next to the old original wood-burning pizza oven was a display of handmade aprons, tapestries, jams, honeys, and cosmetics, all made by various family members.

Chef Andrea is a young man who is strong and quiet, but cheerful. He was very happy to welcome us to his business and home, and he showed us his spotless, sparkling kitchen. If I hadn't known that right outside was a barnyard full of animals, I would have never guessed we were on a farm.

Like all of the chefs before, Chef Andrea prided himself on his ingredients. Almost everything that was served to his guests was grown or produced on his own land, and they were self-sustainable. The guests who visited came to witness farm life, to work, learn, and enjoy the fruits of what comes from what is considered in Italy to be extremely rewarding labor. I was jealous of what they had. Hard work? Absolutely! But the ability to go out your front door and find all you need to sustain the life of yourself and your family is a beautiful thing. I love that Andrea did not take for granted what his family had offered him. A young man with the whole world at his fingertips, he chose to stay at the family farm and help make his family's dream a reality. It's an honest display of dedication. With Andrea's help, his family has been able to become a licensed and official agriturismo. Since then, the business has grown and remains a functioning and lucrative tourist attraction, rather than a way to scrape by in the hopes of making ends meet.

Andrea would settle for nothing less than the best experience for us, and he prepared more dishes than I could count! The first dish was rabbit, and I went into the preparation of the

dish with an open mind. Andrea included the offal of the rabbit as a base for his sauce, explaining that there are many health benefits associated with using the entire animal. Of course, doing so also avoids unnecessary waste. Andrea seasoned the meat with a bouquet of fresh herbs and spices, capers, sun-dried tomatoes, and fragrant garlic and onions. Once the rabbit was simmering in the pan, I honestly looked forward to trying it.

Andrea also prepared mutton stew, a beautiful mutton tenderloin salad with pomegranate reduction, an olive appertivo, lamb with lemon and egg sauce, lamb with artichokes, snails in tomato sauce, fish with an orange glaze, raw fish with fennel and citrus, tortino di verdura, and a lovely pear dessert. You'll find many renditions of Andrea's creations in the recipe section.

When we return to Sardinia, we will look forward to staying at Casa Marmida. Agriturismo is a thriving industry in Italy and should be supported. I am so happy for the experience that we had with Andrea, and I wished we could have stayed longer on Sardinia and included

Casa Marmida as an extended part of our trip. I know that the boys would have loved the experience, and we would have been honored to stay for several days. Andrea is the best of the best, and his hospitality will not be forgotten. We were also given a tour of the guest facilities, which were beautiful and comfortable. Someday, we will go back there to experience Sardinian farm life with the entire family.

I must take these last few sentences to express my gratitude to Marcello. Everyone we met in Italy was kind, genuine, and amazing. But Marcello will be a friend for life. He took us under his wing, gave up precious time with his family, and went above and beyond to help complete strangers. It isn't often that you meet someone as honest and true as Marcello, and this type of experience renews your faith in humanity. He is a solid reminder of how it used to be. We can all learn from Marcello. Be kind for kindness' sake, helpful without asking for anything in return, and be honest about who you are. Thank you, Marcello. We're eternally grateful to have met you.

TRAVEL TIPS AND
TRICKS FOR ITALY

How to Pack

Figuring out how to pack for a month away with children and for different climates is actually quite comical. If you ever embark on a journey such as ours, I suggest you pack as light as possible and stay mindful that you will be doing laundry at least two or three times a week. This is the only way to make it work short of packing twenty suitcases each, especially when lugging children along. Our kids go through clothes like there's no tomorrow, and asking them to keep clean is like asking a monkey not to eat bananas. It's pointless.

I also suggest that you bring a small container of your own laundry soap in case you find yourself in the middle of nowhere without a store nearby. We all brought a limited amount of clothing but made sure that we had layers and at least one warm jacket. The weather was different in every region, so I'm grateful that we planned ahead for this one particular detail. The takeaway? Pack light, bring layers, plan on doing laundry, bring your own laundry soap, and don't forget warm socks!

RECOMMENDED PLACES TO STAY BY REGION

Obviously, we did not travel to every region in Italy, but here is a list of places we stayed that I highly recommend.

Milan

Close to the airport and literally across the street from the train station is the Hotel Ristorante Tre Leoni. This is not so much a hotel as several buildings that have been partitioned into apartments. There are no kitchens in any of the rooms, but the restaurant that is attached to the office is amazing. We found it very easy to eat Paleo meals there. I highly recommend the mixed meat grill, shrimp cocktail, and grilled vegetables. Breakfast, which is included, was not as easy to navigate, but the coffee is good. This is a great place to stay for the night if you have an early flight or train to catch. The hotel offers free shuttle service to the airport and train station. For more information, visit www.hoteltreleoni.com.

While in Bologna, we stayed in a nearby region called Calderara di Reno, which is situated in the countryside of Bologna. We loved the house where we stayed and recommend the location if you truly want a vacation where you can get away from it all. We were very close to the train station, which made it easy to go into the city whenever we wanted. Also, staying in the country gave the boys the opportunity to explore and play outside. You might want to consider renting a car if you stay in this exact location, however. We did not have a car, and while walking back and forth to shops and restaurants was a wonderful experience, there were days when we would rather have not carried several pounds of groceries over a mile each way. For more information about the house, visit: http://www.vacationsfrbo.com/details.php?property_id=80248

We worked directly with the owner of the residence, Alberto Angelici, and he was incredibly kind and helpful. He even picked us up from the train station, took us into town to show us where to eat and shop, and left us two bottles of wine made from his very own grapes.

Bologna

We decided to stay in the town of Pesaro while visiting the Marche region. Pesaro is nestled in a beautiful seaside location and is home to plenty of shopping, sightseeing, and restaurants, but it still has a small town feel. Just from sheer luck, I found Il Pignocco Country House, a farmhouse dating back to the eighteenth century that has been renovated into the beautiful accommodations you'll find today. All of the rooms are equipped with a kitchenette, which allowed us to make the majority of our meals while staying there. The grounds are absolutely gorgeous with a lovely swimming pool and plenty of room to play and stroll, and it is surrounded by an ancient olive grove. The owners of Il Pignocco, Anna and Francesca, are two of the kindest women you will ever meet. While you're there, you must purchase their olive oil. It was some of the absolute best that we sampled while on our trip. For more information, visit www.ilpignocco.it/en/.

The Marche Region

In Rome, you will need an apartment. We could not find a hotel with a kitchen or one large enough to accommodate all of us. Rome is not cheap, I'll tell you that right now, but if you dig deep enough, it's possible to find something that will not entirely empty your pocket book. We ended up staying in an apartment near the Trevi Fountain in the heart of the city. There are so many options to choose from, I can't tell you which is right for you. I would suggest visiting www.VRBO.com and searching for what will work for your family or group. I also suggest staying close to the Trastevere, which is a centrally located, seemingly safe, and a very charming area in Rome.

Rome

Sardinia

Sardinia is absolutely magical, and I would have happily pitched a tent on the beach and stayed there forever. However, it was nice having a roof over our heads and a kitchen to cook in. The house we rented was situated close to the beach and walking distance to a little grocery store and farmers' market. We arrived at the beginning of the winter season, so it felt a bit like a ghost town. But we could tell it would become a bustling and fun beach resort during the summer months. If you want to be really close to the action, I recommend finding a place right in Cagliari. If you like the slower pace and want a hideout by the sea with beautiful grounds and plenty of room to roam, our house's vicinity is your spot. For information about the house and other properties available to rent on Sardinia, visit www.mysardinianvilla.com. You will work directly with Marion, who went above and beyond to help us find accommodations. She even met us at the airport late at night so that we could follow her to our destination. She also left us a huge basket of food, having the foresight that we would be hungry and that nothing would be open that time of night. I highly recommend escaping to Sardinia and contacting Marion to help you find a place to stay, relax, and enjoy the magic of the island.

COMMUNICATION AND NAVIGATION

Having a working cell phone is essential while traveling abroad. We all have iPhones, and prior to leaving the U.S., we called our service provider and requested that they unlock our SIM cards. Be aware that most providers only offer one phone per plan to be unlocked. Once we arrived in Italy, we removed our SIM cards and purchased prepaid Italian SIM cards, which gave us the ability to make local calls and communicate with each other as well. The downside was that we were unable to call back home, but thank goodness for Skype! You can even install the Skype application on your phone, load it with some money, and make your calls back to the States right from your cell phone. This arrangement worked out very well for us. Finding prepaid SIM cards in Italy is very easy, and they can be purchased at almost any convenience store and easily loaded with the typical ten Euro minimum. I think I only used about twenty Euros' worth of calls during the entire four-week trip, which was much less expensive than what my carrier would have charged me for the calls. For more information on using your cell phone while in Italy, visit www.telestial.com.

Before leaving on our trip, we also purchased a GPS unit. This item was priceless. The unit we purchased came loaded with current European maps, and it never steered us wrong. I recommend the TomTom XXL 540TM World Traveler 5-Inch Portable GPS Navigator with Lifetime Traffic & Maps and World Maps found on Amazon.com. I know that this GPS will serve us well as our travels continue around the world. Easy to use, carry, and mount in any vehicle, this unit was a lifesaver as we drove around the vast and sometimes daunting countryside of Italy. The only time our GPS seemed inaccurate was while we were trying to find our apartment in Rome. However, I'm sure our GPS was right on track, but we were just totally confused by Rome's streets.

Public transportation is not too difficult to manage, but for our trip in particular, it was less expensive to rent a couple of cars to drive around the country than it was to purchase multiple train tickets for so many people. If you are traveling alone or as a couple, trains might be the best way to go. But I can't deny that driving gave us the freedom to stop when we wanted and see sights we might not have seen otherwise.

As mentioned, the one place I recommend you do not drive is Rome (unless you're crazy or have a death wish). After our initial drive into Rome to find our apartment and drop off the majority of the team and our luggage, we returned our cars and opted for public transportation. Locate a map from one of the many metro stations, and figure out your route before you head out. You can travel just about anywhere in the city via the metro.

Children under 12 are free on the metro in Rome when traveling with an adult. We felt reasonably safe while using public transportation in Italy, but we were always cautious. Pickpocketing and purse nabbing does happen in Italy, so always keep your wallet in your front pocket or somewhere that can be zipped shut like an inside jacket pocket. Ladies, wear your purse tightly across your body if possible, and always keep it closed and held in front of you. The same is true wherever you travel, not just in Rome. It's responsible to always be aware and mindful of your belongings no matter where in the world you might be. Tourists are often distracted and easily taken advantage of, so don't be caught off guard.

SIGHT SEEING

Rome

The Coliseum and the Roman Forum, Trevi Fountain, the Vatican, St. Peter's Basilica, the Catacombs, and everything else in Rome is a must see. Wander around, and walk inside any church or cathedral you can find. You'll be in awe. Stay for at least a week!

Venice

Amazing, eerie, romantic, and beautiful. I would not want to actually stay in Venice, however. Out of everywhere we visited in Italy, we had the most challenging time finding decent food there. Most of the eateries were expensive and touristy. A day trip was most definitely worth it, though. Venice was a bit tiring to navigate with children, although at age nine, Jaden really enjoyed it. Rowan started to get a little bored and restless and ended up sleeping while we carried him around the crazy, twisting, watery city. The gondola rides are outrageously expensive but totally worth it. If just John and I were to visit Venice alone, I would consider staying at least a night or two in the city, but with a family, I would not.

Such an awesome city, with so much to see and do. I would suggest starting at the Piazza Maggiore. Here, you will find the world's fifth largest basilica and nearby Piazza Nettuno, the home of the Statue of Neptune. Also, down the side streets next to the plaza is the amazing outdoor market that is like stepping back in time. Order red wine from one of the little cafes, sit outside on the streets, people watch, and soak it all in. Also worth seeing is the university, which is the oldest one in the world! The landmark of Bologna is known as The Two Towers, which are medieval structures that hover above the city looming reminders of its ancient history.

Bologna

There are several castles, villages, and beaches to visit in this region, but I highly recommend that you contact Moreno, the guide we used while visiting here. Moreno will be able to build a trip of a lifetime for you and your family, help you find a place to stay, and treat you like royalty. The best part is that his services are incredibly affordable for what he provides. Find Moreno by visiting his website at http://www.lemarcheholiday.net. If you decide to take part in any organized activities, make sure to schedule a truffle hunt!

The Marche Region

Do not go to Sardinia with an agenda. Go to restore, rejuvenate, and relax. The two "big" cities are Cagliari on the south side and Olbia in the north. Both are worth visiting, as each offers its own very distinct cuisine. Of course, all of the restaurants I mentioned in the section on Sardinia are worth hunting down, and be sure to stay a few nights at Casa Marmida! Finally, when in Cagliari, visit the original city walls, and see if you can find the cannonballs still embedded into them.

Sardinia

WHERE AND HOW TO EAT PALEO/GLUTEN-FREE

The best way to eat gluten-free/Paleo in Italy is to find places to stay that have a kitchen. Shopping for food in Italy is an adventure in and of itself. The food is so fresh, and the flavors are fantastic. We had a wonderful time shopping at local grocery stores and farmers markets and cooking up our own creations. Of course, we also ate out on several occasions. We planned ahead, and thanks to the wonderful Internet, we found several restaurants with gluten-free menus. Even restaurants that did not have gluten-free menus were usually easy to navigate. Most restaurants have several meat and vegetable options, and we learned quickly to simply ask "Senza glutine?" to find out if what we were about to order was gluten-free.

Here is a list of places that offered gluten-free dining or which were very accommodating of our needs!

Milan
Hotel Ristoranti Tre Leoni

Bologna
Most of our eating took place either at home or at the Bologna Cooking School with Carlo. However, a quick Google search offers a wide variety of gluten-free dining options. The most popular seems to be Pizzeria Ristorante Pepperoni. They offer gluten-free pizza, grilled meats, salads, and vegetables. Visit their site at www.pepperoni.it.

The Marche Region
Again, we prepared most of our food at Il Pignocco where we were staying, but I highly recommend you visit both Chef Samuele and Chef Davide. We also found a restaurant in Pesaro that offered an extensive gluten-free menu of delicious food.

Osteria Del Parco, Acqualagna, owned by Chef Samuele, www.osteriadelparco.net
Osteria De Gustin, Serrungarina, owned by Chef Virginio, www.dagustin.it

Rome

We ate most of our meals in our apartment and had a wonderful meal prepared for us by Chef Anna Maria and Chef Anna, but it was also easy to find gluten-free restaurants. Here were two of our favorites:

Mama Eat in the Trastavere district, www.mamaeatroma.it
La Soffita, centrally located and totally delicious, www.ristoranterenovatio.it

Sardinia

Amazing food, amazing place. Restaurants you must visit include:

Eno Ristoranti, Chef Davide in Cagliari, www.enorestaurant.it
S'Apposentu, Chef Roberto Petza in Siddi, www.sapposentu.it
Ristorante Lucitta, Chef Clelia in Arbatax, www.ristorantelucitta.com
Agriturismo Casa Marmida, Chef Andrea in Guspini, www.casamarmida.it

RECIPE ORIGINS
things you need to know,
and what about the dairy and the grains?

The vast majority of recipes in this book are my own renditions of the recipes that I learned from the wonderful chefs, farmers, and home cooks in Italy. Under each recipe, I list where I learned it or where I found my inspiration. You will also find renditions of traditional Italian dishes that we researched and sampled from various establishments or from extensive studying while abroad. Some recipes are from regions we did not actually visit. That's where the research came in. So, the recipes in this book are Paleo with a "Sarah spin," while remaining as authentic as possible.

Now, what about all that dairy? Everyone knows that cheese is the bee's knees in Italy, but some Paleo folks avoid dairy altogether while others enjoy some fermented dairy in the form of cheese, yogurt, sour cream, or kefir. Still other Paleo people feel just fine eating full-fat dairy like heavy cream or butter now and then. I live in the camp of "do what works best for you." My family always avoids food that contains gluten, but now and then we will eat some fermented dairy, heavy cream, and butter. If you eat dairy products from time to time, I make suggestions to add some cheese or cream. You can always grate some Parmesan on top of just about anything in this book, and you will not be disappointed.

If you avoid all dairy due to an allergy, intolerance, or autoimmune condition, don't fear. Every recipe that calls for anything dairy-related includes an alternative. So, yes, the recipes

can all be made 100% Paleo with one exception. The Tiramisu calls for mascarpone cheese, and there's no way around it. Without the mascarpone cheese, I would not do justice to the Italian chef who taught me the dish, and I couldn't find another way to make it even close to the real deal. I apologize for this in advance, but I offer several other desserts to fit your dietary needs.

What you will never find in this book are grains. There are absolutely NO grains used in any of the recipes whatsoever. Even the gnocchi is grain-free.

One final note about the desserts. Please remember that desserts are treats. For most people, eating sweets on an everyday basis, even grain-free and made with otherwise healthy ingredients, is not conducive to good health. Furthermore, the traditional Italian meal rarely ends with a giant dessert, but rather with a small and humble one. To reflect this ideology, the portions and serving sizes in this section will not be huge. So, be prepared to double any dessert recipe if you're feeding a crowd.

THE #1 ITALIAN CUISINE RULE –
Take Your Time and Make It With Love

A handful of the recipes that you are about to dive into are not necessarily "everyday" recipes. A few require a bit more time and preparation, so pay close attention to the suggested prep and cooking times before you fire up your burners. The Italian way of cooking is often slow and requires time and patience rather than thirty-minute meals made in a snap! None of the recipes are overly complicated, however. You will also find several meals that you can make quickly in my typical "Everyday Paleo" style. Highlight the recipes you know you can make quickly for those hectic weeknight meals, and mark the ones that will be reserved for weekends, less busy days, parties, or celebrations.

One thing I can assure you: Whatever you make, the recipes in this book are straight from my heart. The recipes have all been created with a fierce passion for real food and attention to detail so that you can recreate what I was able to bring home from the chefs I met in Italy.

I wish you all the time in the world to relax, reconnect, and live the best life possible with the ones you love the most. Eat, live, and love well, and as always, enjoy! Ciao!

INGREDIENTS, KITCHEN TOOLS, AND RESOURCE GUIDE

I have listed specific ingredients, gadgets, and ideas below with instructions, tips, and resources to make navigating your way through the recipes in this book easier and less time-consuming. I include my thoughts based on commonly asked questions, as well as my experiences while writing the book. I also list resources where you can order some of these ingredients online. Most of what I suggest will not be hard to find in major grocery stores, and you can use whatever brands you can find. My recommendations are simply based on brands that I use and trust. Depending on where you live, some ingredients might be harder to find than others, which is also why I make online ordering recommendations. You can always visit EverydayPaleo. com for support or questions about all things Paleo.

INGREDIENTS
Sarah's Recommendations

Almonds, Almond Flour, Almond Butter

My favorite brand of everything almond is Ammin Nut Company. Their products can be ordered at www.amminnut.com. For the gnocchi, however, I recommend using finer ground almond flour such as Bob's Red Mill or Honeyville. Feel free to use any almond flour, butter, or nut of your choice, but try to find organic or as unprocessed as possible.

Animal Fats: Lard, Duck Fat, Tallow

The premium source of all things animal fat is Fatworks, which offers high quality animal fat from grass-fed and pasture-raised animals. To order their premium lard, duck fat, and tallow, visit:

http://fatworks.wazala.com/ or https://www.facebook.com/fatworks.

Butter

I recommend using butter from grass-fed cows, and one of the best brands is Kerrygold. It also happens to be the easiest to find–it's available at Trader Joe's, Costco, Whole Foods, and most major grocery and health food stores.

Coconut Milk

Most coconut milk comes in a can, and I recommend Native Forrest brand. They do not use BPA in their cans, and I like the way their milk tastes. I also recommend Chaokoh coconut milk. They do not use guar gum, which can sometimes cause irritation for people with digestive issues. Both brands can be found online or in most major grocery stores and health food stores.

Cured Meats:

Prosciutto di Parma, Pancetta, Salami, Bresaola, Coppa

Applegate Farms offers coppa, salami, pancetta, and prosciutto made from humanely raised pork with minimal processing and ingredients. If you cannot find pancetta in your area, bacon is the perfect substitute. Most gourmet food stores or even major grocery stores carry cured meats, but I suggest you read labels to make sure you buy the most minimally processed brands. You can also order gourmet cured meats online from Applegate Farms and at sources such as:

www.applegate.com
www.gourmetfoodstore.com
www.dibruno.com
www.igroumet.com

Ghee

For those of you who have an autoimmune condition, I recommend that you avoid all dairy products. An alternative to butter is ghee–clarified butter that is free of any remaining milk solids, leaving behind only the golden, delicious fat. I have tried many different brands of ghee, and you may already have your own favorite. But Mama Sattva Ghee is the brand I love the most based on taste, quality, and knowing that it comes from grass-fed cows. You can order this ghee at www.mamasattva.com.

Fresh Herbs such as Basil, Oregano, Rosemary, Thyme, Mint, Sage and Italian Parsley

Italian parsley is the flat-leaf variety that looks like cilantro. You can use the curly-leafed parsley if you can't find the Italian type, but I prefer the milder taste of Italian parsley. Fresh herbs are usually used in the recipes, and I love to grow my own! All you need is a small planter box and a windowsill, so even with limited space it's easy to grow fresh herbs. If you buy them from a store, keep them fresh for several days by storing them in a glass of water in the refrigerator, just make sure to change the water in the glass every couple of days. If you want to grow your own, check out this site: www.farmfreshliving.com/Growing_Organic_Herbs.html

Extra Virgin Olive Oil

In most parts of Italy you will find chefs and home cooks alike cooking with extra virgin olive oil. However, because olive oil can break down under high heat and oxidize, I prefer to sear meat and to sauté in animal fat, butter, or ghee. I do feel comfortable heating extra virgin olive oil when used at the end of your cooking time; for example, in a sauce or to flavor food before serving, in which I know the olive oil will not be heated enough to reach it's smoke point and oxidize. You will find that I use plenty of delicious extra virgin olive oil in the majority of the recipes in this book to add flavor; but in most recipes I suggest other fats for high heat cooking in place of the often-used extra virgin olive oil.

For extra virgin olive oil that you can trust, I recommend finding a local source in your area or ordering from the following trusted suppliers:

www.tropicaltraditions.com

www.luceerooliveoil.com

www.kasandrinos.com

Heavy Cream

Heavy cream can be used as an alternative to coconut milk if full-fat dairy agrees with you and you don't have an autoimmune condition. I recommend finding a source of heavy cream that comes from grass-fed cows, if possible.

Meat such as Italian Sausage, Beef, Lamb, Rabbit, Pork Belly, Etc.

US Wellness Meats is an amazing supplier of grass-fed and pasture-raised meats. You can find everything on their website from sausage to rabbit. To order, visit: www.grasslandbeef.com.

For other grass-fed meats, I also highly recommend the following:
www.massanaturalmeats.com
www.txbarorganics.com

Mutton

I had to list this separately because it's by far the most difficult ingredient in this book to find. If you locate a source for mutton in the U.S., please email me because I was hard-pressed to find a supplier. Nevertheless, in order to be true to the authenticity of these recipes, I listed mutton as an option, but lamb or beef can be substituted.

Sun-Dried Tomatoes

Sun-dried tomatoes are usually easy to find in grocery stores. Just read the label to make sure they're packed only in extra virgin olive oil with no additives that look unfamiliar. I highly recommend Bella Sun Luci, a brand that should be easy to find, or you can order it online at www.mooneyfarms.com.

White Sweet Potatoes

White sweet potatoes can sometimes be difficult to find. If you are unable to locate them, I believe that organic, regular white–fleshed potatoes are not problematic for most healthy individuals and can be used as a substitute. However, if you have an autoimmune condition or a severe fat loss goal, regular white potatoes are best avoided. You can also substitute traditional orange-fleshed sweet potatoes or what are often referred to as "yams" in place of the white variety.

KITCHEN TOOLS

All of the following items are found in the Everyday Paleo Amazon Store or at most kitchen supply and gourmet kitchen stores.

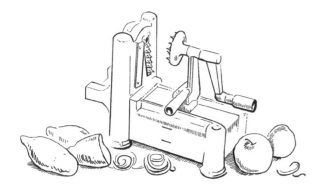

Spiral Vegetable Slicer
Makes perfect vegetable noodles every time.

Food Mill
This tool is very helpful to remove the skins and seeds from tomatoes.

Potato Ricer
Great to break up the sweet potatoes for the gnocchi recipe and the sweet potato soufflé recipe.

Microplane Zester/Grater

A must have for the Italian kitchen and great for lemon garlic, ginger, nutmeg, and much, much more!

Pastry Cutter

Essential for making gnocchi and so helpful to scoop up all those chopped, minced, diced, and sliced veggies.

Handheld Immersion Blender

Wonderful kitchen tool used to easily blend soups and sauces while still in the pan. Cuts down on cleanup and time spent in the kitchen.

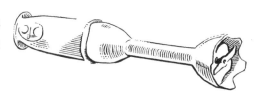

Food Scale

You will appreciate this handy tool when measuring out the exact amount needed for items like cubed sweet potatoes and other quantities for recipes that are required by weight.

ANTIPASTI

Green Olives
with Sun-Dried Tomatoes
olive verdi condite con pomodori secchi

Prep Time: 10 minutes   Serves: 5

When we arrived at Casa Marmida on the island of Sardinia to work with Chef Andrea, it was the last stop of our trip, and we were starting to become a little bit homesick. Chef Andrea, however, made us feel like we were home and welcomed us with warmth, food, and genuine hospitality. Amongst many other delicious dishes, he offered this simple, yet lovely appertivo. Serve this to your guests with a few other antipasto dishes while you prepare the rest of your Italian meal!

10 ounces cured green olives

2 tablespoons sun-dried tomatoes packed in extra virgin olive oil, minced

1 garlic clove, minced

1 tablespoon fresh Italian parsley, minced

1 tablespoon extra virgin olive oil

1. Drain the olives, rinse them with water, and place them in a small mixing bowl.

2. Add the sun-dried tomatoes, garlic, Italian parsley, and extra virgin olive oil.

3. Mix well, and serve as a snack!

Turkey Breast Antipasto

antipasto di petto di tacchino

*Prep Time: **15 minutes*** *Serves: **4-5***

Almost too simple to be special, this was an antipasto served to us in the Marche region by Chef Samuele after our amazing truffle hunt. This dish made the recipe section of my book because it's a true testament to how something simple can be "spot on" and how a lot of fuss can be too much. This is an amazingly tasty appetizer or light lunch and can be whipped up in just a few minutes. As pictured below, this antipasto can also be made with thinly sliced smoked duck.

½ pound cooked turkey breast, thinly sliced

3 cups baby arugula

1 cup shredded carrots

¼ cup extra virgin olive oil or to taste

2 tablespoons balsamic vinegar or to taste

Sea salt and black pepper to taste

1. On a large serving platter, arrange a layer of the thinly sliced turkey breast.

2. Top the turkey evenly with the arugula.

3. Sprinkle on the shredded carrots.

4. Drizzle with the extra virgin olive oil and balsamic vinegar.

5. Season with sea salt and black pepper, and serve small portions on plates.

Stuffed Squash Blossoms
fiori di zucca ripieni

Prep Time: 45 minutes Cook Time: 15 minutes Serves: 6-7

This was the first recipe that Chef David of Eno made for us on the beautiful island of Sardinia, and I knew immediately that this man knew what he was doing in the kitchen. This is a seasonal dish that you will only be able to make when squash blossoms are in bloom, but trust me, it's worth waiting for the right time of year to enjoy this special treat. Your guests will be impressed with the beauty and taste of this refined, lovely, scrumptious appetizer. If you are unable to find squash blossoms in your area, you can order them when in season from www.marxfoods.com.

1 tablespoon duck fat, butter, or ghee

4 ounces pancetta, finely chopped

2 cups zucchini, finely chopped

½ cup green onions, finely chopped

½ cup walnuts, finely chopped

Sea salt and pepper to taste

15-20 squash blossoms

Extra virgin olive oil

Tomato Cream (page 164)

1. Preheat your oven to 325°F.

2. In a large skillet heat the duck fat, butter, or ghee over medium heat. Add pancetta and cook until almost crispy.

3. Add the zucchini and green onions and sauté until the zucchini is tender but not mushy.

4. Add the walnuts and sauté for another 2-3 minutes and season to taste with sea salt and black pepper.

5. Transfer the stuffing mixture from the pan to a separate bowl and place in the refrigerator until cool.

6. To prepare the squash blossoms, gently reach into the blossom and pinch out the stamen or pistol. Twist off the stem if desired but you may also leave intact for visual appeal. Gently rinse under cool water and place the blossoms on paper towels to dry.

7. Once the blossoms are dry and the stuffing is cool, it's time to stuff the squash blossoms.

8. Place the contents of the stuffing into a pastry bag and gently fill the opening of each blossom until almost full. The petals at the end of the blossom should be able to close around the stuffing.

9. Place each stuffed blossom into a large baking dish.

10. Drizzle all of the stuffed blossoms with a little bit of extra virgin olive oil and bake uncovered for 10-12 minutes.

11. Serve with the Tomato Cream as a sauce.

Fried Squash Blossoms

fiori di zucca fritti

Prep Time: 30 minutes   Cook Time: 4 minutes   Serves: As many as you like

I made Fried Squash Blossoms for the first time with Big Carlo in Bologna and he informed me that this is a very typical Italian antipasto loved throughout the country. I recreated this dish by using tapioca flour rather than rice flour, and I am still amazed at how easy and delicious these little crispy treats turned out. I recommend frying them in beef tallow, but if you only have coconut oil on hand, they will still be terrific. But trust me, the beef tallow adds a special savory deliciousness that you will not want to miss.

TEMPURA BATTER

1 cup tapioca flour

¼ cup mineral water

2 eggs

Pinch of sea salt

Beef tallow or coconut oil for frying

Squash blossoms (as many as you like)

Sea salt

1. To prepare the squash blossoms, gently tear the side of one blossom from the top down to the base of the petal and remove just the petals from the stem of the blossom and discard the stem, stamen, and pistols. The blossom should now be able to lay flat.

2. In a medium-mixing bowl, whisk together the tempura batter ingredients.

3. In a deep skillet or sauté pan, add about ½ cup beef tallow or coconut oil and heat over medium-high heat.

4. The oil should be hot enough to sizzle when you add the squash blossoms.

5. Dredge one squash blossom at a time into the tempura batter and add gently to the hot oil. Fry for 1-2 minutes per side in the hot oil or until the batter starts to crisp and brown.

6. Remove blossoms from the hot oil with metal tongs, let them drain on paper towels, and then sprinkle them with a little sea salt before serving.

7. Serve immediately with the Tomato Cream (page 164) or Pesto (page 167) as a dipping sauce or eat just as they are.

Italian Shrimp Cocktail

cocktail di gamberi

Prep Time: 15 minutes   Yield: 1¼ cups

This classic Italian rendition of shrimp cocktail was one of the first things I ate after we landed in Milan and fumbled our way to Hotel Ristoranti Tre Leoni. The creamy dressing is delightful served with any seafood of your choice, but my favorite is prawns, cooked quickly and cooled. You can make it as spicy or mild as you like. Don't forget the squeeze of lemon!

2 tablespoons tomato paste

½ tablespoon apple cider vinegar

½-1 tablespoon honey

1 cup homemade mayo (see below)

Tabasco sauce, salt, and lemon juice to taste

1 pound large shrimp or prawns, shells removed and deveined

1. Whisk all of the ingredients together, and chill the sauce in the fridge.

2. Serve with chilled, cooked shrimp or prawns.

3. To cook the shrimp or prawns, bring a large pot of water to boil along with one lemon cut into rounds.

4. Drop the shrimp into the boiling water. When they turn pink and rise to the top, they are done.

5. Remove the shrimp immediately from the hot water into an ice bath to stop the cooking process and cool the shrimp.

6. Serve with the cocktail sauce and more lemon slices for garnish.

MAYO

2 egg yolks

2 tablespoons apple cider vinegar

1 teaspoon yellow mustard

1 teaspoon sea salt

¼ teaspoon cayenne pepper

2 cups light-tasting olive oil

Homemade Mayo

Prep Time: 10 minutes   Yield: 2½ cups

1. In a medium-sized mixing bowl, add the egg yolks, vinegar, mustard, salt, and cayenne pepper.

2. Using a hand held mixer set on medium speed, begin to beat together the contents of the mixing bowl for five seconds.

3. Without stopping the mixer, slowly, slowly, slowly drizzle in the olive oil.

4. Once the mayo starts to emulsify (or thicken) you can start to pour it a bit faster, but do not dump all the olive oil in at once—be patient or the emulsification will separate.

5. Continue to mix the mayo with the hand held mixer until the olive oil is all combined and the mayo has reached your desired consistency.

Chopped Chicken Salad
insalata di pollo

Prep Time: 45 minutes   Cook Time: 15 minutes   Serves: 2-3

Another fast and easy appetizer or salad, this twist on the typical chopped salads that you find in the States has a great combination of flavors. The rosemary and mushrooms cooked together give a beautiful bouquet to an otherwise "normal" chicken salad. I know this one will be a go-to for your fast lunch, dinner, or as antipasto before dinner.

2 tablespoons lard, butter, or ghee

I cup mushrooms, sliced

I tablespoon fresh rosemary, minced

I cup green beans, diced

Salt and pepper to taste

4 cups baby arugula, or other salad greens of your choice

I cup cooked chicken, diced

I cup cherry tomatoes, quartered

I cup red grapes, halved

Chives, chopped

Italian parsley, chopped

¼ cup slivered almonds

Extra virgin olive oil to taste

Balsamic vinegar to taste

1. In a medium skillet, heat the lard, butter, or ghee over medium heat.

2. Add the mushrooms to the hot skillet, and sauté for 7-10 minutes. Add the rosemary to the mushrooms, and sauté for another 1-2 minutes.

3. Remove the mushrooms from the pan and set aside.

4. Add the green beans to the same pan, and sauté for 5-7 minutes or until tender.

5. Season the green beans with a little salt and pepper, and remove them from the pan, setting them aside.

6. To arrange the salad, fill the bottom of a large salad bowl with the baby arugula. On top of the arugula, arrange the chicken, green beans, mushrooms, cherry tomatoes, and grapes in sections as seen in the picture.

7. Top the salad as desired with chopped chives, parsley, slivered almonds, extra virgin olive oil, balsamic vinegar, salt, and pepper.

Vegetable Quiche
tortino di verdura

Prep Time: 40 minutes   Cook Time: 50 minutes   Serves: 5-6

Dreamy, delicious, flavorful, fresh—these are all words that came to mind when Chef Andrea made us his version of vegetable quiche. Serve this for breakfast or brunch, and wow your family and guests. This meal is as visually stunning as it is tasty! If you include a bit of dairy in your diet, I suggest adding one cup of cubed pecorino cheese before baking.

1 medium eggplant, thinly sliced into rounds (approximately 10-12 ounces)

1 cup tomatoes, finely diced

1 red bell pepper, seeds removed, peeled and finely diced

Sea salt and black pepper to taste

1 cup pecorino cheese, cubed, optional

12 eggs

1 garlic clove, minced

2 tablespoons fresh basil, diced

2 tablespoons fresh Italian parsley, diced

1. Preheat your oven to 350°F.

2. Heat a large skillet over medium heat, and place the thinly sliced eggplant rounds into the dry skillet. Cook for approximately 2-3 minutes per side. You'll have to do several batches of these, as they all won't fit into the pan at once.

3. Place a layer of the eggplant slices on the bottom of a 9" x 13" baking dish.

4. Evenly sprinkle on the diced tomatoes.

5. Add another layer of eggplant slices.

6. Evenly spread the diced red bell pepper.

7. Add one last layer of eggplant slices if there are any left, and sprinkle some sea salt and black pepper over the top.

8. If you are using the pecorino cheese, evenly sprinkle the cubed cheese on top of all of the vegetables.

9. In a large mixing bowl, whisk the eggs together with the garlic, basil, and Italian parsley.

10. Pour the egg mixture evenly over the vegetable layers in the baking dish.

11. Cover tightly with foil, and bake for 30 minutes in the preheated oven.

12. Remove the foil, and bake for another 15-20 minutes or until the eggs are set all the way through.

Mushroom Antipasto
antipasto di funghi

Prep Time: 30 minutes   Cook Time: 10 minutes   Serves: 6-8

Mushrooms are almost considered sacred in Italy, and when in season, the porcini mushrooms are a prized possession. While in the beautiful Marche region visiting Osteria Da Gustin, Chef Virginio made us a porcini mushroom antipasto, focusing on the earthy freshness of the mushrooms that were harvested just that morning. This is my own twist on the dish using either baby portobello (crimini) or porcini mushrooms.

12 ounces crimini or porcini mushrooms

2 tablespoons lard, butter, or ghee

3 ounces prosciutto, diced

Extra virgin olive oil

Balsamic Reduction (page 157)

¼-½ cup Italian parsley, diced

Sea salt and black pepper to taste

1. Using a damp paper towel, gently clean the mushrooms.

2. Thinly slice the mushrooms lengthwise, and arrange them in a layer on a serving platter. Set aside. (The mushrooms are served raw.)

3. In a small skillet, heat the lard, butter, or ghee over medium-high heat.

4. Add the diced prosciutto to the hot skillet, and sauté until crispy.

5. Sprinkle the crispy prosciutto evenly over the sliced mushrooms.

6. Drizzle the mushrooms and prosciutto with extra virgin olive oil and Balsamic Reduction.

7. Sprinkle the diced Italian parsley evenly over the entire dish, season to taste with sea salt and black pepper, and serve.

Zucchini Quiche
tortino di zucchine

Prep Time: 45 minutes   Cook Time: 1 hour   Serves: 5-6

In Rome, we explored ancient ruins, wandered the narrow, historically rich streets, and ate some of the most amazing food on our journey. This is my take on a recipe taught to me by Anna Maria. If you are not a huge fan of anchovies, this dish is delicious without them, or you can put half on one side of the casserole for the anchovy lovers and leave half without!

2 tablespoons butter or ghee

1 small white onion, sliced

2-3 anchovy fillets finely diced, optional

4 medium zucchini squash, thinly sliced lengthwise, about ¼-inch in thickness, using a mandoline is easiest

3 garlic cloves, minced

¼ cup Italian parsley, diced

3 ounces pancetta, diced

12 eggs, whisked

Sea salt to taste (Only use if you decide not to use the anchovies; do not use with the anchovies, or your dish will be way too salty.)

1. Preheat your oven to 350°F.

2. In a medium skillet, heat the butter or ghee over medium heat, and sauté the onions until browned.

3. Add the diced anchovies to the onions, and sauté for another 3-4 minutes.

4. Remove the onions and anchovies from the pan, and set aside.

5. Add the sliced zucchini to the same pan, and gently cook, turning occasionally until tender.

6. Evenly layer the cooked zucchini in a 9" x 13" baking dish. Top with the onion and anchovy mixture, garlic, and Italian parsley, and set aside.

7. In the same skillet, cook the pancetta over medium heat until crispy, and set aside.

8. Pour the eggs over the veggies in the baking dish, and sprinkle the top with the cooked pancetta.

9. Cover and bake in the preheated oven for 30 minutes.

10. Uncover and bake for another 15-20 minutes or until the eggs are set all the way through.

Italian Pickled Vegetables
giardiniera

Prep Time: 40 minutes   Pickling Time: 2 days   Yield: 2 quarts

This classic twist on typical Italian pickled vegetables is now a staple in our house! It's easy to make, and delicious as an antipasto or condiment. Feel free to try different veggie options, or experiment with different herbs and spices to create your own unique version. Have fun, and enjoy!

1 cup cauliflower florets (cut into small pieces)

3-4 celery ribs, cut into small sticks

3 small carrots, cut into small sticks

1 red bell pepper, cut into slices

1 green bell pepper, cut into slices

1 yellow bell pepper, cut into slices

1 red onion, cut into slices

4 garlic cloves, smashed

2 teaspoons red pepper flakes, divided, optional

SOLUTION

1½ cups white wine vinegar

½ cup extra virgin olive oil

2 tablespoons black peppercorns

⅓ cup sea salt

2 tablespoons dried oregano

2 teaspoons celery seeds

1. Fill 2 1-quart jars with even amounts of cut up cauliflower, celery, carrots, red bell pepper, green bell pepper, yellow bell pepper, onion, and garlic.

2. To make it spicy, add 1 teaspoon per jar of red pepper flakes.

3. In a small saucepan, add all of the solution ingredients, mix well, and bring to a simmer.

4. As soon as the solution starts to simmer, remove the pan from the heat, and let it sit for 5 minutes.

5. Pour equal amounts of the solution into the two jars filled with vegetables.

6. Add water to each jar to fill the rest of the way, close tightly with the lids, and shake gently.

7. Refrigerate for at least 2 days before eating. These pickled veggies will last for several weeks in the fridge (but I promise you'll eat them quickly!)

Roasted Garlic

aglio arrosto

Prep Time: 15 minutes   Cook Time: 30-40 minutes   Yield: As much as you like

Simple and essential, everything tastes better with creamy, aromatic roasted garlic. Serve with any of the steak or lamb dishes, and use it as an ingredient in any of the bruschetta's.

½ tablespoon lard, butter, or ghee per garlic bulb

Whole garlic bulbs (as many as you like)

Sea salt to taste

1. Preheat your oven to 375°F.

2. In a medium-sized skillet, heat the lard, butter, or ghee over medium-high heat.

3. Meanwhile, slice off just the top of the garlic bulbs, exposing the cloves inside.

4. Place the garlic bulbs, cut side down, in the hot pan and cook until brown, about 3-5 minutes.

5. Remove the garlic from the pan, and place the cut side up in a baking dish.

6. Roast uncovered in the preheated oven for 30-40 minutes or until the cloves are easily removed from the bulb and fork tender or easy to mash. Salt to taste.

Salmon Carpaccio

carpaccio di salmone

Prep Time: 20 minutes Serves: 3-4

This eye-catching and tasty antipasto can be served as a light lunch or breakfast. Personally, I like to make the Salmon Carpaccio for brunch. I also like to pair it with Vegetable Quiche (page 88) for a fun weekend meal or holiday celebration.

4 ounces smoked salmon

¼ cup extra virgin olive oil

1 tablespoon red onion, minced

2 tablespoons lemon juice

1 tablespoon Italian parsley, minced

2 tablespoons capers

Pinch of sea salt and black pepper

1.

Thinly slice the smoked salmon into strips, and place them in a small mixing bowl.

2.

Add the remaining ingredients, and gently toss together and serve.

Tomato Bruschetta
bruschetta al pomodoro

Prep Time: 30 minutes   Serves: 4-5

The classic Italian fresh tomato bruschetta (pronounced brus'ketta) has an origin that dates back to the 15th Century. It is traditionally served on bread, so I had to think of a different vessel in order to make it Paleo. After several different trials, our family agreed that it tasted the best served on top of slices of hard salami, but feel free to experiment! Try serving this classic antipasto on slices of cucumber, bell pepper strips, or even roasted slices of eggplant!

1 tablespoon fresh or Roasted Garlic (page 96), minced

2 tomatoes, diced (about 1 cup)

2 tablespoons red onion, minced

¼ cup fresh basil, chopped

1 tablespoon balsamic vinegar

3 tablespoons extra virgin olive oil

¼ cup Italian parsley, chopped

Sea salt and black pepper to taste

1.

In a large bowl, mix all ingredients together, and serve on top of cucumber, bell pepper, or hard salami slices.

Artichoke Bruschetta
bruschetta ai carciofi

Prep Time: 20 minutes   Serves: 4-5   *Serve on cucumber or hard salami slices

This artichoke bruschetta is a unique twist on the classic tomato version. Again, serving it on slices of hard salami was our favorite. Make sure you double or triple this recipe to feed a crowd. It's delicious and sure to go fast!

1 cup finely diced, artichoke hearts from a jar or can, drained

1 tablespoon red onion, minced

3 tablespoons homemade mayonnaise (page 84)

¼ cup red bell pepper, finely chopped

2 tablespoons fresh basil, minced

1 garlic clove, minced, or 1 teaspoon Roasted Garlic (page 96), minced

1.

In a large bowl, mix all ingredients together, and serve on top of hard salami or cucumber slices.

Mixed Antipasto
antipasto misto

Prep Time: 30 minutes   Serves: 6-8

Quick, easy, and classic, this salad can be made one hundred different ways, so please consider this more of an idea than an actual recipe. Nothing says Italy like delicately aged prosciutto and fresh basil, so make sure that whatever variation you try, you always include these two staples.

1 red bell pepper, seeds removed and cut into rounds

1 yellow pepper, seeds removed and cut into rounds

1 bunch basil leaves, cut into strips

4 ounces prosciutto, thinly sliced

4 ounces salami, thinly sliced

4 ounces Bresaola, thinly sliced

3-4 hardboiled eggs, sliced into rounds

1 cup Kalamata olives, chopped

1 cup sun-dried tomatoes not packed in olive oil, julienne-sliced

Extra virgin olive oil

Balsamic vinegar or Balsamic Reduction (page 157)

1.

Arrange all ingredients on a platter for folks to choose and share.

2.

Serve with balsamic vinegar or Balsamic Reduction (page 157) and extra virgin olive oil for drizzling or dipping.

Caponata

Prep Time: 45 minutes Cook Time: 30 minutes Serves: 6-8

Savory, slightly sweet, and comforting, this classic Sicilian dish can also be served as a side dish with any of the meat recipes in this book. Try serving it on top of grilled steak, chicken, or fish, tossed with greens for a salad, or as an antipasto with sliced veggies instead of bread.

3-4 tablespoons lard, tallow, butter, or ghee

1 small red onion, finely diced

4 cups eggplant, diced

3 celery stalks, diced

3 garlic cloves, minced

½ cup pitted green olives, diced

3 tablespoons capers

⅔ cup golden raisins

¼ cup pine nuts

2 small tomatoes, diced (about 1 cup)

¼ cup fresh basil, diced

¼ cup fresh Italian parsley, diced

1 cup sun-dried tomatoes packed in olive oil, julienne-sliced

2 tablespoons red wine vinegar

¼ cup extra virgin olive oil

Sea salt and black pepper to taste

1. In a large skillet, heat the lard, tallow, butter or ghee over medium-high heat.

2. Add the onion, and sauté until translucent.

3. Turn the heat down to medium and add the eggplant and celery, and sauté until the eggplant is soft (about 10 minutes).

4. Add the garlic, olives, capers, golden raisins, pine nuts, tomatoes, basil, Italian parsley, sun-dried tomatoes, and red wine vinegar, and cook, stirring often, for another 7-10 minutes.

5. Add the extra virgin olive oil, mix well, and serve on top of sliced bell peppers, cucumbers, or hard salami slices. Add salt and pepper to taste.

Stuffed Mushrooms
funghi ripieni

Prep Time: 40 minutes   Cook Time: 15-20 minutes   Serves: 6-8

The best things in life often come in small packages, and these little bundles of goodness are a great example of that. The Italian lifestyle is all about good food, friends, and family, so I suggest serving these for your next family gathering. Remember to slow down, savor the moment, and enjoy the ones you love the most.

6 ounces white or crimini mushrooms

2 tablespoons lard, butter, or ghee

½ cup yellow onion, finely chopped

1 pound mild Italian sausage, casings removed

1 cup celery, finely chopped

½ cup red bell peppers, finely chopped

1 tablespoon fresh oregano leaves, minced

2 garlic cloves, minced

2 egg yolks

3 teaspoons fresh Italian parsley, minced

Balsamic Reduction (page 157), optional

1. Gently clean the mushrooms with a damp paper towel.

2. Remove the stems from the mushrooms, and finely chop just the stems.

3. Preheat your oven to 350°F.

4. Place the cleaned mushrooms, caps down, on a baking sheet, and set aside.

5. In a large skillet, heat the lard, butter, or ghee over medium-high heat, add the onion, and sauté for 4-5 minutes.

6. Add the sausage to the skillet, and cook until it has browned.

7. Add the celery, red bell peppers, and finely chopped mushroom stems, and cook for another 5-7 minutes.

8. Add the oregano and garlic, and cook for another 2-3 minutes.

9. Place the meat mixture into a food processor, and pulse until everything is finely chopped but not "mush."

10. Add the 2 egg yolks and the minced Italian parsley to the meat mixture, and stir.

11. Spoon the meat mixture into each mushroom cap, and bake uncovered in the oven for 15-20 minutes.

12. Serve drizzled with Balsamic Reduction, if desired.

Radicchio with Pancetta Dressing

radicchio con pancetta croccante

Prep Time: 15 minutes   Cook Time: 15 minutes   Serves: 4-5

Before our trip to Italy, I would use radicchio as a garnish to make my plate look pretty or to add some color to my salad. But now, I have a deeper appreciation for this ingredient. Pairing the slightly bitter lettuce with the richness of pancetta and olive oil and the sharpness of vinegar is scrumptious. Served as an antipasto or a side dish, I know you'll also grow to appreciate radicchio for more than just a touch of color on your plate.

2 tablespoons duck fat, butter or ghee

¼ cup shallots, minced

4 ounces pancetta, diced

2 garlic cloves, minced

3 tablespoons extra virgin olive oil

2 tablespoons white wine vinegar

1 tablespoon dried or fresh oregano leaves

Sea salt and pepper to taste

1 head small radicchio, torn into bite-sized pieces

1. In a medium skillet, heat the duck fat, butter or ghee over medium heat.

2. Add the shallots to the hot pan, and sauté until translucent.

3. Add the diced pancetta, and sauté until crisp.

4. Add the garlic, and sauté for about 2 minutes.

5. Turn the heat to low, and add the extra virgin olive oil, white wine vinegar, and oregano.

6. Whisk, taste, and season with the salt and pepper. Serve the dressing drizzled over the torn radicchio leaves.

Drunken Cauliflower

cavolfiori al vino bianco

Prep Time: 20 minutes   Cook Time: 20 minutes   Serves: 5-6

The little bit of heat from the crushed red peppers makes this spin on cauliflower absolutely divine. It is delicious served with the Steak with Savory Onions and Grapes on page 220.

1 tablespoon lard, butter, or ghee

4 ounces pancetta, diced

1 small cauliflower, cut into bite-sized florets

2 garlic cloves, cut in half

½ cup white wine

¼ cup extra virgin olive oil

2 bay leaves

⅛ teaspoon red chili peppers, crushed (or more to taste)

¼ cup Italian parsley, minced

Sea salt and pepper to taste

1. In a large sauté pan or skillet, melt the lard, butter, or ghee over medium-high heat.

2. Add the pancetta to the pan, and brown.

3. Turn the heat down to medium, add the cauliflower and garlic, and sauté for 3-4 minutes.

4. Add the white wine, and let it reduce for 2-3 minutes.

5. Cover, and cook on low for another 5-7 minutes.

6. Add the extra virgin olive oil, bay leaves, chili peppers, Italian parsley, salt and pepper, stir well, and cook for another 2-3 minutes.

Artichokes with Salsa Verde

carciofi in salsa verde

Prep Time: 10 minutes   Cook Time: 30-40 minutes   Yield: ½ cup of Salsa Verde

This Salsa Verde is beyond yummy and can be used as a sauce or condiment for just about anything. The artichoke is a coveted veggie in Italy, however, so pairing the two together is a match made in culinary heaven.

SALSA VERDE

½ cup Italian parsley

1 tablespoon capers

2½ tablespoons onions or shallots, minced

1 garlic clove

1 anchovy fillet

⅛ teaspoon red pepper flakes

¼ cup extra virgin olive oil

1 tablespoon white wine vinegar

2 tablespoons heavy cream or full-fat canned coconut milk

Sea salt to taste

Lemon wedges for serving

As many artichokes as you would like.

1. Use as many artichokes as you like. Place a steamer basket in a large soup pot, and add 3-4 cups of water.

2. Trim the stems and the tops of the leaves from the artichokes, and place them in the steamer basket.

3. Cover the pot, and bring the water to a boil over high heat.

4. Turn the heat down to medium, and steam the artichokes for 30-40 minutes or until the leaves are easily pulled from the artichokes.

5. Meanwhile, combine all of the ingredients for the Salsa Verde in a food processor, and blend until completely smooth. Season to taste with sea salt.

6. Serve as a dip for the steamed artichokes, along with lemon wedges.

PIZZE

Pizza

While in Italy, we had the pleasure of sampling several gluten-free pizzas. We also learned about traditional pizzas and their history. Italian pizzas are smaller and usually served individually—toppings can be anything from fresh tomatoes and oregano to seafood. I have a basic almond meal pizza crust recipe that you can find in **Everyday Paleo,** *but after sampling the pizza crust created by Tammy Credicott in* **Paleo Indulgences,** *I knew this was the crust that would do justice to the authentic Italian pizza. Thank you, Tammy, for giving me permission to use your crust recipe. Please be sure to check out her awesome books,* **Paleo Indulgences** *and* **The Healthy Gluten-Free Life** *at: www. thehealthyglutenfreelife.com.*

Pizza Crust

*From **Paleo Indulgences** by Tammy Credicott*

Prep Time: *10 minutes*   **Cook Time:** *15-25 minutes depending on toppings*

Yield: *1 9-inch crust*

1. Preheat your oven to 425°F.

2. Place the ingredients for the yeast mixture in a small bowl and mix. Let sit about 4-5 minutes to activate and become foamy.

3. Meanwhile, place the dry ingredients in a medium bowl and whisk to combine.

4. Add the yeast mixture and the wet ingredients to the dry ingredients. Mix well with a hand mixer.

5. Scoop the mixture onto a parchment-lined baking sheet, using a rubber spatula to spread evenly in a circle.

6. Bake 9-10 minutes. Remove from the oven, carefully flip crust over with a spatula, top with any of the following suggested sauce and toppings and bake another 5-10 minutes or until toppings are hot. Slice and enjoy!

YEAST MIXTURE

¼ cup warm water

2 teaspoons raw honey

2 teaspoons active dry yeast

DRY INGREDIENTS

¾ cup almond flour

3 tablespoons coconut flour, sifted

⅔ cup arrowroot flour

pinch sea salt

WET INGREDIENTS

1 egg

2 teaspoons extra virgin olive oil

1 teaspoon raw apple cider vinegar

The Toppings!

The typical tomato sauce for authentic Italian pizza is very basic. I suggest using San Marzano whole canned tomatoes. Use a spoon to break up the tomatoes and spread the sauce on the crust of the pizzas that call for tomato sauce. The pizzas that call for extra virgin olive oil are to be made without tomato sauce. Simply drizzle the pizza crust evenly with plenty of high quality extra virgin olive oil prior to adding the suggested toppings. The toppings of the pizza and the herbs add the flavor you will need—the simpler the better for these delicious pizzas! Use as many or as few toppings as you like, experiment, and enjoy. The toppings suggested are typical of what you will find in various regions of Italy at authentic pizzerias. Although not listed, feel free to add fresh mozzarella and/or Parmesan cheese as desired.

PIZZA 1

Extra virgin olive oil, tomato slices, thinly sliced garlic cloves, fresh oregano leaves, sprinkle of sea salt

PIZZA 2

Tomato sauce, sprinkle of dry oregano, thinly sliced ham, sliced mushrooms, sliced artichoke hearts, chopped kalamata olives

PIZZA 3

Tomato sauce, sprinkle of dry oregano, thinly sliced mushrooms, anchovies, thinly sliced ham, sliced black olives

PIZZA 4

Tomato sauce, arugula, thinly sliced prosciutto

PIZZA 5

Pesto Sauce (page 167), thinly sliced mushrooms, thinly sliced eggplant, cooked and crumbled mild Italian sausage, tomato slices

PIZZA 6

Tomato sauce, thinly sliced ham, thinly sliced crimini mushrooms, basil leaves, 1 egg

Top the pizza evenly with suggested toppings except the egg. Bake for 5 minutes. Remove the pizza and crack the egg in the middle of the pizza. Bake for another 5-10 minutes or until the egg whites are cooked and the yolk is still a bit runny. Slice and enjoy!

PIZZA 7

Tomato sauce, sliced zucchini, thinly sliced eggplant, spinach leaves, thinly sliced purple onions, thinly sliced red bell peppers, cooked and crumbled mild Italian sausage, drizzle of extra virgin olive oil

PIZZA 8

Extra virgin olive oil, prosciutto, sun-dried tomatoes, sliced black olives, basil leaves, thinly sliced purple onions

PIZZA 9

Extra virgin olive oil, sliced artichoke hearts, sun-dried tomatoes, cooked and crumbled spicy Italian sausage, basil leaves

PIZZA 10

Tomato sauce, cooked and crumbled mild Italian sausage, thinly sliced ham, diced and cooked pancetta, capers, thinly sliced fennel

PRIMI PIATTI

First Courses, Sauces, Side Dishes & Soups

Noodles

PRIMI
PIATTI
First Courses,
Sauces,
Side Dishes
& Soups

I suggest four types of noodles to enjoy with the different sauce recommendations you will find throughout this book.

Spaghetti Squash: This is truly "natures pasta" and is as delicious as it is nutritious. Spaghetti squash has a mild taste and pairs well with any sauce in this book. I especially love it with the Classic Bolognese (page 184). Make sure as you're cooking to watch your squash closely until you are used to preparing this vegetable. Spaghetti squash is great when done just slightly al dente, but when you overcook it and it turns into mush, it's not all that enjoyable.

How to prepare a spaghetti squash in a microwave:

1. My favorite way is to simply poke a few holes in the skin of the squash with a knife and microwave on high for 8-20 minutes, depending on the size of the squash and the power of your microwave.

2. I suggest turning the squash over every five minutes for even cooking. Once the squash is easily pierced with a steak knife, it's done!

3. Remove the squash and let it sit for 10 minutes or so to cool.

4. Cut the squash in half and gently remove the seeds. Use a regular dinner fork to scrape out the strands of squash.

How to bake spaghetti squash:

1. Preheat your oven to 375°F.

2. Cut the squash in half lengthwise and scoop out the seeds.

3. Place the squash, cut side up, in a large baking dish and add ½ cup of water to the bottom of the dish.

4. Bake uncovered for 30-40 minutes dependent on the size of your squash. The squash is done when easily pierced with a fork.

5. Use a fork to scrape out the strands of squash!

Sweet Potato or Zucchini Noodles: These two options are my boys' favorites, mostly because of the preparation. In the kitchen equipment section of this book I recommend a Spiral Vegetable Slicer, which is the greatest discovery our family has made in a long time! This tool makes perfect vegetable noodles and my kids absolutely love to help! To prepare the vegetable pasta, simply cut the ends off of a peeled sweet potato, put in place, and turn the handle, and out comes beautiful, long noodles. Same with the zucchini; cut off the ends, place in the machine, and turn.

How to prepare the zucchini or sweet potato noodles:

1. Make the noodles with the Spiral Vegetable Slicer.

2. Boil a large pot of water.

3. Add the zucchini or sweet potato noodles and quickly blanch in the water for 1 minute. Do NOT overcook or the sweet potato noodles will fall apart and become mush.

4. Serve topped with your favorite sauce.

5. Alternatively, you can sauté the zucchini or sweet potato noodles with the fat of your choice in a large wok or sauté pan until al dente. Add the sauce right to the pan with the noodles, sauté for another minute or two, and serve!

Cappello's Grain Free Pasta—Cappello's grain free noodles are made with the following ingredients: almond flour, cage-free eggs, tapioca flour, potato starch, xanthan gum, and sea salt. In my opinion, that's pretty amazing for actual pasta! The texture and taste are truly delicious and although I consider these noodles a treat and we typically always use vegetables as a vessel for our sauces, it's nice to have an alternative for those special occasions. You can find Cappello's Grain Free Pasta online at: http://cappellosglutenfree.com/.

PRIMI
PIATTI
First Courses,
Sauces,
Side Dishes
& Soups

PRIMI
PIATTI

*First Courses,
Sauces,
Side Dishes
& Soups*

Sweet Potato Soufflé
soufflé di patate dolci

Prep Time: 45 minutes   Cook Time: 30-40 minutes   Yield: 14-16 Soufflés

I made potato soufflé with Chef Samuele at his osteria in Aqualagna following our epic truffle hunt. I loved Samuele's perspective that simple ingredients put together the right way make food taste divine. This is my twist on his recipe that called for lots of milk and cheese. These dairy-free soufflés use white sweet potatoes instead of regular, and I added some crispy pancetta for texture and flavor. You can use heavy cream instead of the coconut milk if you tolerate full-fat dairy. Otherwise, the coconut milk version is just as tasty (if not better!) Our whole family loves these, and the boys request them often for breakfast. Note: This recipe makes approximately 15 soufflés. If you're not planning to feed a crowd, you might want to cut the recipe in half.

14-16 baking ramekins

Coconut oil, butter, or lard for greasing the ramekins

4 pounds white sweet potatoes, peeled and cubed into even large chunks

8 ounces pancetta, finely chopped

6 eggs

1 13.5-ounce can full-fat coconut milk or 1½ cups heavy cream

1½ teaspoons sea salt

½ teaspoon black pepper

1. Preheat your oven to 350°F.

2. Grease the ramekins, and set them aside.

3. Boil the sweet potatoes for 20 minutes or until they are soft all the way through.

4. Drain the potatoes, and let them sit until they are cool enough to handle.

5. Meanwhile, in a medium-sized skillet, cook the pancetta over medium-high heat until browned and crispy. Set aside.

6. Into a large bowl, push the cool potatoes through a potato ricer, or mash them with a potato masher.

7. Add the eggs and coconut milk or heavy cream to the potatoes, and mix well.

8. Add the sea salt, pepper, and cooked pancetta, and mix the ingredients into the potatoes and milk.

9. Evenly pour the potato mixture into the greased ramekins, and place them on a baking sheet.

10. Place the baking sheet with the ramekins into the preheated oven, and cook for 30-40 minutes or until a toothpick inserted into one of the soufflés comes out clean.

PRIMI
PIATTI

*First Courses,
Sauces,
Side Dishes
& Soups*

Italian Roasted Sweet Potatoes

patate dolci al forno

Prep Time: 20 minutes   Cook Time: 30-40 minutes   Serves: 5-6

Simple yet delicious, this is my version of this classic Italian side dish, using sweet potatoes instead of white potatoes. Rustic and satisfying, the rosemary with the sweet potatoes offers a yummy twist on this staple. We ate roasted Italian potatoes with Chef Virginio at Osteria Da Gustin, and he paired them with the Herbed Chicken with Pancetta (page 128). I highly recommend that you do the same! Out of this world scrumptious!

2 pounds white sweet potatoes, peeled and diced

¼ cup duck fat, tallow, butter, or ghee, melted

2 teaspoons fresh rosemary, minced

Sea salt and pepper to taste

1. Preheat your oven to 400°F.

2. In a large mixing bowl, toss the diced sweet potatoes with the melted duck fat, tallow, butter, or ghee along with the fresh rosemary.

3. Evenly spread the potatoes on a baking sheet, and bake for 30-40 minutes or until the potatoes are browned and fork tender. Stir halfway through the cooking time.

4. Season with salt and pepper to taste, and serve.

PRIMI
PIATTI

First Courses,
Sauces,
Side Dishes
& Soups

Mushrooms with Tomato

sugo ai funghi

Prep Time: 15 minutes   Cook Time: 25 minutes   Serves: 4-5

I've already mentioned the delightful mushrooms in Italy, and this classic recipe is fantastic served with the Slow Cooked Pork Belly (page 248) or with any other meat dish in this book. The surprising combination of mint, parsley, and shallots with the creaminess of the mushrooms and acidity of the tomatoes is delicious.

2 tablespoons duck fat, lard, butter, or ghee

⅓ cup shallots, minced

12 ounces (5-6 cups) wild mushrooms, sliced

2 garlic cloves, minced

½ tablespoon fresh mint, minced

1 tablespoon fresh Italian parsley, minced

Sea salt and pepper to taste

¼ cup tomato sauce

1. In a large skillet, heat the duck fat, lard, butter, or ghee over medium heat, and sauté the shallots for 4-5 minutes.

2. Add the mushrooms, and cook for another 3-4 minutes.

3. Add the garlic, mint, and Italian parsley, and sauté just until the garlic is fragrant.

4. Season with salt and pepper, add the tomato sauce, and cook for another 10-15 minutes.

PRIMI
PIATTI

First Courses,
Sauces,
Side Dishes
& Soups

Cabbage Salad

cavoli in insalata

Prep Time: 20 minutes   Serves: 5-6

I made this light and refreshing salad with Chef Davide at Vineria Ristorante Eno. Please eat Cabbage Salad with whatever protein you like, but the duo of the Fish Burger (page 224) along with the crunch and sweetness of the cabbage, apple, and pomegranate flavors is perfection!

4 cups green cabbage, finely shredded

1 medium apple, diced

1 cup pomegranate seeds

1 cup golden raisins

¼ cup extra virgin olive oil

2 tablespoons lemon juice

Sea salt and pepper to taste

1. In a large mixing bowl, combine the shredded green cabbage, diced apple, pomegranate seeds, and golden raisins, and mix well.

2. In a small mixing bowl, whisk together the extra virgin olive oil and lemon juice, drizzle the dressing over the salad, and toss together.

3. Season with salt and pepper to taste.

Egg with Asparagus

uova e asparagi

Prep Time: 25 minutes   Cook Time: 20 minutes   Serves: 4-5

It's a crazy sounding combination, I know, but trust me on this one! Fresh herbs, creamy egg yolk, and tender asparagus just work together! Serve this as a side dish, antipasto, or lunch. I love this dish paired with the Stuffed Mushrooms (page 104) as a fun and creative meal.

6 eggs

2 tablespoons lard, butter, or ghee

3 tablespoons extra virgin olive oil

1 tablespoon lemon juice

1 tablespoon fresh thyme leaves, minced

¼ cup fresh Italian parsley, chopped

Sea salt and pepper to taste

1 bunch asparagus (or approximately 2 pounds)

1. In a medium-sized saucepan, cover the eggs with water, and bring to a boil over high heat.

2. Turn the heat down to medium, and simmer the eggs for 6 minutes.

3. Transfer the eggs to a bowl of ice water to stop the cooking process, and let them cool for 4-5 minutes.

4. Meanwhile, fill a large soup pot halfway with water, and bring it to a boil over high heat. This will be used to cook the asparagus.

5. While waiting for the water to boil, peel the eggs, cut them in half, and remove the yolks, which may be slightly runny in the center.

6. Finely mince the egg yolks and the egg whites, keeping them separate from one another.

7. In a medium-sized skillet, melt the lard, butter, or ghee over medium heat.

8. Add the minced egg yolks, and whisk them into the melted oil in the pan (it will be lumpy).

9. Turn the heat to low, and add the extra virgin olive oil, lemon juice, thyme, half of the minced egg whites, and the Italian parsley. Season to taste with salt and pepper.

10. Remove the egg sauce from the heat, and set it aside.

11. By now, your water should be boiling for the asparagus. Drop the asparagus into the boiling water, and cook for 3-4 minutes until tender but still crisp.

12. Using cooking tongs or a slotted spoon, remove the asparagus from the water to a serving platter.

13. Top the asparagus with the egg sauce, and sprinkle on the remaining minced egg whites. Serve immediately.

PRIMI
PIATTI

*First Courses,
Sauces,
Side Dishes
& Soups*

Eggplant Parmesan
melanzane alla parmigiana

Prep Time: 45 minutes   Cook Time: 15 minutes   Serves: 5

You can keep the cheese or skip it, but this simple version of Eggplant Parmesan is impressive. I made this dish with Chef Davide at Vineria Ristorante Eno and was surprised at his take on the typically heavy, cheese-laden, baked in goopy-goodness recipe. The fresh tomato sauce and simply prepared eggplant is almost too easy to be delicious, but it's really out of this world. My kids call this dish "Italian Nachos," and we love them without the cheese just as much as we love them with a sprinkle of grated Parm! Don't forget the drizzle of extra virgin olive oil at the end!

1 medium-sized Italian eggplant, thinly sliced into rounds using a mandoline slicer

3-4 cups Basic Tomato Sauce (page 162)

Extra virgin olive oil

Grated Parmesan cheese, optional

Fresh basil leaves, diced, for garnish

1. Line a baking sheet with parchment paper, and preheat your oven to 350°F.

2. To sweat out some of the moisture from the eggplant slices, place the thinly sliced pieces of eggplant onto paper towels, sprinkle them with salt, and let them sit for 10-15 minutes.

3. Turn the eggplant slices over, sprinkle them with a little more salt, and let them sit for another 10 minutes.

4. Meanwhile, make the Basic Tomato Sauce found on page 162.

5. While the tomato sauce is simmering, place the eggplant pieces on a parchment-lined baking sheet.

6. Bake the eggplant in the preheated oven for 5 minutes, turn them over, and continue to bake them for another 5 minutes or until they start to brown. Once the eggplant pieces are done, it's time to plate the dish!

7. Start by placing one piece of the eggplant onto a plate, spoon on a layer of the tomato sauce, add another piece of eggplant, and then more sauce until you have at least 4 layers of eggplant and sauce. Build each plate individually before serving, or to make it easier, layer the eggplant slices alternating with the sauce in a small serving dish to serve at the table.

8. Drizzle the finished dish with a little bit of extra virgin olive oil.

9. Top with freshly grated Parmesan cheese, if desired, and diced fresh basil.

PRIMI
PIATTI

*First Courses,
Sauces,
Side Dishes
& Soups*

Vegetable Broth

brodo di verdure

Prep Time: 30 minutes   Cook Time: 1-2 hours
Yield: Approximately 5 cups broth

At Casa Marmida with Chef Andrea on the island of Sardinia, the first thing we noticed when we walked into his kitchen was the simmering pot of vegetable broth on the stove. It was delicious magic, and he added a bit of this broth to several of his dishes. Now I must have this broth available as often as possible in my own kitchen. I love the uniqueness of the sun-dried tomatoes with the parsley.

1 small white onion, cut into large chunks

4 small carrots, cut into large chunks

4 celery stalks, cut into large chunks

3 garlic cloves, cut in half

2 tablespoons sun-dried tomatoes

6 cups cold water

¼ cup fresh Italian parsley, chopped

Sea salt to taste

1. In a large soup pot, place the onion, carrots, celery, garlic, and sun-dried tomatoes.

2. Cover the vegetables with the cold water, and place the pot over high heat.

3. Bring the pot to a boil, turn the heat to low, add the Italian parsley, and simmer for 1-2 hours.

4. Season with sea salt, and strain the broth from the vegetables.

5. Store in an airtight glass container in the refrigerator up to seven days, and use as needed.

PRIMI
PIATTI

First Courses,
Sauces,
Side Dishes
& Soups

Beef Broth
brodo di carne

Prep Time: 45 minutes Cook Time: 2-6 hours
Yield: Approximately 5-6 cups of broth

Beef and chicken broth are must-have staples, especially for making the Ossobuco (page 222) and the "Risotto" alla Milanese (page 198). Use these broths also as a base for soups, stews, or just to drink on a cold day. You'll find several recipes in this book that call for beef or chicken broth, and making your own is the best option. Super food at its finest, the broth is full of vital nutrients and minerals and much tastier than store bought. It's worth the extra bit of effort.

2 pounds beef chunks and beef bones (knuckle bones, if possible)

4 carrots, cut into chunks

4 celery stalks, cut into chunks

1 yellow onion, cut into chunks

2 garlic cloves

2 tablespoons apple cider vinegar

6 cups water

Sea salt to taste

1. Preheat your oven to 400°F.

2. Line a baking sheet with foil. Place the beef bones and beef chunks on the baking sheet, sprinkle with sea salt, and roast in the oven for 30-45 minutes.

3. When the beef is done, add the beef and all of the drippings from the baking sheet to a large soup pot.

4. Add the carrots, celery, onion, garlic, apple cider vinegar, and water to the pot, and bring the broth to a boil over high heat.

5. Turn the heat to low, and simmer for at least 2 hours up to 6 hours, adding more water occasionally, as necessary. Add salt to taste.

6. Strain the broth, and store it in glass containers in your refrigerator up to 7 days.

7. You can also make this in a slow cooker. Simply follow all of the same directions except put everything in your slow cooker, and cook on low for 6-8 hours.

Chicken Broth
brodo di pollo

PRIMI
PIATTI

*First Courses,
Sauces,
Side Dishes
& Soups*

Prep Time: 15 minutes   Cook Time: 1-2 hours
Yield: Approximately 5-6 cups of broth

1. In a large soup pot, heat the lard, butter, or ghee over medium-high heat.

2. When the oil is nice and hot, add the chicken pieces, and brown for 3-5 minutes on each side.

3. While the chicken is browning, cut the carrots, celery, and onion into even sized large chunks.

4. Once the chicken is browned, add the chopped veggies and garlic cloves.

5. Add the apple cider vinegar and water, and bring the broth to a boil over high heat.

6. Turn the heat to low, and simmer for 1-2 hours.

7. Season to taste with sea salt and black pepper.

8. Pour the broth through a strainer, and store it in the refrigerator in airtight containers.

9. Use any leftover chicken meat for salads or just to eat!

3 tablespoons lard, butter, or ghee

1½ pounds chicken parts, bone-in and skin on

4 carrots, cut into chunks

4 celery stalks, cut into chunks

1 yellow onion, cut into chunks

2 garlic cloves, halved

2 tablespoons apple cider vinegar

6 cups water

Sea salt and black pepper to taste

PRIMI
PIATTI

First Courses,
Sauces,
Side Dishes
& Soups

Pumpkin Cream with Prawns

crema di zucca con gamberi

Prep Time: 1 hour Cook Time: 35 minutes Serves: 4-5

This is my take on Chef Davide's pumpkin cream with prawns recipe. The prawns Chef Davide used were pulled straight from the Mediterranean, red and succulent, and served intact with the head and all. Real food served as fresh as possible is an Italian tradition that I hope to keep alive by passing these recipes on to you.

PUMPKIN CREAM

2 tablespoons butter or ghee

2 cups leeks, finely diced

1 small sugar pumpkin, peeled and cubed, yields approximately 6 cups

Chicken Broth (page 141), enough to just cover the cubed pumpkin

1 tablespoon fresh oregano leaves

3 tablespoons extra virgin olive oil

Sea salt to taste

PRAWNS

3-4 tablespoons butter or ghee

12 large prawns, shells removed and deveined

1 tablespoon white wine

1 tablespoon Garlic Oil (page 158)

Sea salt to taste

OPTIONAL

Minced fresh oregano leaves or chives for garnish

1. In a large soup pot, heat the butter or ghee over medium heat.

2. Add the leeks, and sauté them until tender, about 5-7 minutes.

3. Add the cubed pumpkin and enough Chicken Broth to cover the pumpkin. Raise the heat to high, and bring the pot to a boil.

4. Turn the heat to low or medium-low, and let simmer for approximately 20 minutes or until the pumpkin is fork tender.

5. Add the oregano leaves and let the pot simmer another 3-5 minutes.

6. Remove the pot from the heat, and blend the pumpkin mixture until completely smooth using a handheld immersion blender or transfer to a food processor and process until smooth.

7. Add the extra virgin olive oil, and mix well.

8. Season to taste with sea salt, and set the mixture aside.

9. Now, it's time to prepare the prawns. In a large skillet, melt the butter or ghee over medium-high heat.

10. Once the butter is hot, add the cleaned prawns, and sauté them quickly for about 1 minute, turning often.

11. Add the wine to the hot pan with the prawns, and stir. Cook for another 1-2 minutes or until the prawns are pink and firm.

12. Turn the heat off, and add the Garlic Oil and a little bit of salt. Toss the prawns in the oil to coat.

13. Serve the pumpkin cream in soup bowls topped with 2-3 prawns per person.

14. Drizzle each serving with a little bit of the cooking oil from the prawn pan and minced fresh oregano leaves or chives, if desired for garnish.

PRIMI
PIATTI

First Courses,
Sauces,
Side Dishes
& Soups

Mussels & Clams Soup

zuppa di cozze e vongole

Chef Davide, with his culinary genius, made this dish for us. The white wine and homemade Chicken Broth are the key ingredients to this recipe, and, of course, finding mussels and clams as fresh as possible is equally important! Adding in the Basic Tomato Sauce at the end and plenty of good extra virgin olive oil pulls it all together. Impress your guests with this one!

1 pound fresh mussels

1 pound fresh clams

¼-½ cup white wine

2 cups Chicken Broth (page 141)

2 garlic cloves, minced

2 cups Basic Tomato Sauce (page 162)

¼ cup extra virgin olive oil

½ cup fresh Italian parsley, minced

Sea salt to taste

1. Place the mussels and clams in a large soup pot.

2. Turn the heat to medium-high, and add the white wine to the hot pot.

3. Bring the wine to a simmer for 2-3 minutes.

4. Add the Chicken Broth and minced garlic to the wine, mussels, and clams. Mix well, cover, and cook for another 4-5 minutes or until all of the clams and mussels are open.

5. Add the Basic Tomato Sauce, extra virgin olive oil, Italian parsley, and a little bit of sea salt to the pot. Mix well, and remove the pot from the heat.

6. Use a ladle to serve into large soup bowls.

Vegetable Soup
zuppa di verdure

Prep Time: 35 minutes   Cook Time: 30 minutes   Serves: 5-6

During our day trip to Venice, one of the most magical places I have ever been, we found a café tucked down a little side street and sat outside, watching the sights that you'll only see in this particular spot in the universe. We ate the typical grilled steak and arugula, a huge salad, shared a fresh lobster, and tried their vegetable soup. We couldn't get enough of the fresh flavors of the soup, enhanced by the oregano and thyme leaves! This is my version of the lovely soup that we savored in Venice.

½ cup yellow onion, finely diced

2 tablespoons butter or ghee

3 garlic cloves, minced

2 cups Chicken Broth (page 141)

3 cups cold water

2 cups carrots, diced

2 cups celery, diced

2 cups green beans, diced

2 cups zucchini, diced

1 tablespoon fresh oregano leaves, minced

1 tablespoon fresh thyme leaves, minced

Sea salt and black pepper to taste

Extra virgin olive oil

1. In a large soup pot, sauté the onion in the butter or ghee over medium-high heat until translucent.

2. Add the garlic and sauté just until fragrant.

3. Add the Chicken Broth and water, and bring the liquid to a simmer over medium-high heat.

4. Add the carrots, celery, and green beans. Turn the heat to medium-low, and simmer for 15-20 minutes or until the veggies are tender.

5. Add the zucchini, oregano, and thyme, and simmer for another 7-10 minutes or until the zucchini is tender.

6. Season with salt and pepper to taste. Drizzle in a little extra virgin olive oil to taste, and serve.

PRIMI
PIATTI

*First Courses,
Sauces,
Side Dishes
& Soups*

Fish Soup
zuppa di pesce

Holy cow, Chef Roberto is truly a ninja in the kitchen! Not surprising since he is a two-time recipient of a Michelin Star, and people come from far and wide to eat his food and learn from the master himself. I still can't believe that Chef Roberto was kind enough to take an entire day to cook with me and share his passion and love for the slow food movement. From farm-to-table, or even his own backyard-to-table, the freshness of ingredients is the secret to his success. In order to experience his talent firsthand, of course, you should take a trip someday to the island of Sardinia, visit the little town of Siddi, find his restaurant, S'Apposentu, and spend a culinary evening that you will never forget. In the meantime, you can make this meal at home, which is my own spin on his delectable fish soup.

I pound sushi-grade ahi fillet

½ cup sun-dried tomatoes, finely chopped

½ cup basil, finely chopped

½ cup chives, finely chopped

6 cups Chicken Broth (page 141)

I cup leeks, finely chopped

I cup carrots, finely chopped

I cup celery, finely chopped

¾ cup radishes, finely chopped

I teaspoon fresh ginger, grated

Sea salt and black pepper to taste

Fresh basil, chopped, for garnish

Fresh chives, chopped, for garnish

1. Dice the ahi into ½-inch cubes, and place even amounts of the raw fish into 4-5 soup bowls.

2. Top the fish with even amounts of the sun-dried tomatoes, basil, and chives.

3. Sprinkle the fish with some sea salt and set the bowls aside.

4. In a large soup pot, add the Chicken Broth, leeks, carrots, and celery.

5. Bring the pot to a boil over high heat.

6. Turn the heat to medium-low, and simmer for 10-12 minutes or until the veggies are tender but still al dente.

7. Add the radishes, and cook for another 3-4 minutes.

8. Add the fresh ginger, stir well, and season with additional sea salt and black pepper to taste.

9. Turn the heat to high, and bring the pot to a boil.

10. Using a ladle, pour 1-2 ladles full of the hot broth and veggies over the raw fish in each soup bowl. The hot liquid will instantly cook the small pieces fish.

11. Serve immediately, garnished with a bit more fresh chopped basil and chives.

PRIMI
PIATTI

First Courses,
Sauces,
Side Dishes
& Soups

Meatball and Escarole Soup

zuppa di scarola e polpette

Prep Time: 45 minutes   Cook Time: 30 minutes   Serves: 5-6

This is a fun version of the classic Italian Wedding Soup. My kids love the little meatballs, and until my trip to Italy, I didn't think a whole lot about escarole. Now, I love to cook with this beautiful ingredient. This easy, yet satisfying, soup is sure to become a family favorite.

2 tablespoons lard, butter, or ghee

1 yellow onion, diced

3 medium carrots, diced

4 cups Chicken Broth (page 141)

2 pounds ground pork

3 garlic cloves, minced

1½ teaspoons sea salt

1 medium head escarole

⅓ cup Italian parsley, chopped

Pinch red pepper flakes or more to taste

2 tablespoons extra virgin olive oil

Sea salt and black pepper to taste

1. In a large soup pot, heat the lard, butter, or ghee over medium-high heat, and sauté the onion until translucent.

2. Add the carrots and Chicken Broth, and bring the soup to a simmer.

3. Meanwhile, in a medium-sized mixing bowl, mix the pork, garlic, and sea salt together with your hands.

4. Once the Chicken Broth is simmering, use your hands to form the meat into small meatballs about half the size of a golf ball, and drop them into the soup.

5. Tear the escarole leaves into bite-sized pieces, and add them to the soup.

6. Let the soup simmer for 10-12 minutes or until the meatballs are done all the way through.

7. Add the Italian parsley, red pepper flakes, and extra virgin olive oil, and gently stir.

8. Season to taste with salt and pepper, and serve.

PRIMI
PIATTI

*First Courses,
Sauces,
Side Dishes
& Soups*

Minestrone Soup
minestrone

Prep Time: 40 minutes   Cook Time: 45 minutes   Serves: 5-6

It's simply not an Italian cookbook without minestrone, the soup that is about as old as Italy itself. This particular recipe for minestrone is one of my favorites. I don't know if it's the touch of sweetness from the sweet potatoes paired with the bacon or the freshness from the pesto, but my entire family looks forward to this as a yummy first course to any meal.

1 pound pancetta or bacon, diced

1 yellow onion, diced

2 garlic cloves, minced

4 celery stalks, diced

4 small carrots, diced

3 cups white sweet potatoes, diced

4 cups Chicken Broth (page 141)

1 28-ounce can San Marzano whole tomatoes

½ cup Pesto (page 167)

Salt and pepper to taste

½ cup Italian parsley, finely diced, for garnish, optional

1. In a large soup pot, brown the pancetta or bacon over medium-high heat until it starts to brown.

2. Add the diced onion, and cook for 5-7 minutes.

3. Add the garlic, celery, carrots, and sweet potatoes, and cook for another 3-4 minutes.

4. Add the Chicken Broth and tomatoes, and cook until the veggies are soft, stirring occasionally (approximately 20 minutes).

5. Meanwhile, make the Pesto.

6. Stir in the Pesto, season to taste with salt and pepper, and serve garnished with Italian parsley, if desired.

PRIMI
PIATTI

*First Courses,
Sauces,
Side Dishes
& Soups*

Creamy Carrot Fennel Soup

zuppa di finocchi e crema di carote

Prep Time: 20 minutes   Cook Time: 30 minutes   Serves: 4-5

This is the one dish inspired by our farm stay adventure in Abruzzo. The soup that we had there was not overly flavorful, but I loved the concept. This rendition is utterly fabulous, if I do say so myself! The richness from the coconut milk or heavy cream adds depth, and the bite of the Balsamic Reduction and saltiness from the pancetta is just plain great.

4 large carrots, diced (about 3 cups)

1 large fennel bulb, diced (about 1½ cups)

2 garlic cloves, halved

3 cups Vegetable Broth (page 138)

1 cup full-fat canned coconut milk or heavy cream

Sea salt to taste

½ cup pine nuts, toasted

4 ounces pancetta, diced

Balsamic Reduction (page 157), optional

1. In a medium soup pot or saucepan, add the carrots, fennel, garlic, and Vegetable Broth. Bring to a simmer over medium-high heat.

2. Turn to medium-low, and simmer the vegetables until tender, about 15-20 minutes.

3. Add the coconut milk or heavy cream, stir, and let simmer another 3-5 minutes.

4. Using a handheld immersion blender or food processor, blend the mixture until smooth. Season to taste with sea salt.

5. Meanwhile, in a small skillet, cook the pancetta over medium-high heat until crispy.

6. To toast the pine nuts, place in a dry skillet and stir or shake the pan constantly over medium high heat until they start to brown. Remove quickly from the heat once browned in order not to burn.

7. Serve the soup topped with the toasted pine nuts, the crispy pancetta, and if desired, a drizzle of Balsamic Reduction.

PRIMI
PIATTI
First Courses,
Sauces,
Side Dishes
& Soups

Herb Mixture
condimento alle erbette

Prep Time: 15 minutes   Yield: ½ cup herb mixture

This is the herb mixture that was taught to me by Chef Virginio at Osteria Da Gustin in the Marche region. He used it for the Herbed Chicken with Pancetta, but don't stop with just this one recipe! You can use this herb mixture with any protein, or add it to sauces and soups. Just be sure to mince all of the ingredients finely enough that it looks almost like a roughly chopped pesto.

3 tablespoons fresh sage, minced

3 tablespoons fresh rosemary, minced

3 tablespoons fresh bay leaves, minced

6 garlic cloves, minced

1.

Mince all of the ingredients together, and use the mixture as a rub on chicken, pork, fish, or lamb. You can use a food processor to speed the chopping time.

Balsamic Reduction
riduzione di aceto balsamico

PRIMI
PIATTI

*First Courses,
Sauces,
Side Dishes
& Soups*

Prep Time: 15 minutes   Yield: ½ cup balsamic reduction

This is a staple that you'll find as a garnish and ingredient in many of the recipes in this book. Make enough ahead of time to have plenty on hand. It's great to drizzle on grilled meats or to accompany any of the antipasti or salads. Note: Balsamic Reduction will last for years, just simply store it in a glass container in your pantry!

1 cup balsamic vinegar

1.

In a small saucepan, bring the vinegar to a simmer over medium-high heat.

2.

Turn the heat to medium-low, and simmer until it is reduced by half and thick like syrup, whisking often during the process so that the vinegar does not burn.

PRIMI
PIATTI

First Courses,
Sauces,
Side Dishes
& Soups

Garlic Oil
olio all'aglio

Prep Time: 10 minutes Yield: ½ cup garlic oil

Chef Davide suggested to routinely make Garlic Oil and Basil Oil to add to recipes, and I have taken his advice. I love this new ingredient in my kitchen. Whether I'm making an Italian meal or anything else, adding some Garlic or Basil Oil gives it extra flavor and brightness. Remember to always use your fresh Garlic Oil right away and discard any leftovers. It's not safe to store garlic in oil and must be eaten fresh.

½ cup extra virgin olive oil

3-5 garlic cloves

1.

Finely mince the garlic cloves and whisk together with the oil. Important note: Use all of the garlic oil immediately and do NOT store for later use! Garlic stored in olive oil at room temperature or even in the refrigerator poses the risk of botulism as garlic is grown in the ground where there is Clostridium Botulinum. Oxygen kills the bacterium but because the oil does not allow oxygen in, it does pose a risk that is not worth taking. So enjoy your garlic oil but eat it immediately after preparation.

Basil Oil

olio al basilico

Prep Time: 10 minutes   Yield: 1½ cups basil oil

PRIMI
PIATTI

*First Courses,
Sauces,
Side Dishes
& Soups*

I cup extra virgin olive oil

I cup basil leaves

1.

In a food processor or blender, blend the oil and basil together until smooth. Store in the refrigerator up to 5 days. The olive oil will harden when kept cool, so before using scoop out desired amount with a spoon and let it sit at room temperature until it becomes liquid again.

PRIMI
PIATTI

First Courses,
Sauces,
Side Dishes
& Soups

Béchamel Sauce
besciamella

Prep Time: 20 minutes   Cook Time: 40 minutes   Yield: Approximately 3 cups

This is one recipe you might have thought impossible after switching to a Paleo lifestyle, but this version of Béchamel sauce is creamy and satisfying. It opens the door to many possibilities in the kitchen that otherwise would have been impossible. You'll find this recipe used in my Lasagna (page 202) and with my Mushroom Meatballs (page 204).

1 pound white sweet potatoes (typically 1 large sweet potato)

¼ cup butter or ghee

2 cups full-fat canned coconut milk or heavy cream

¼ teaspoon nutmeg

½ teaspoon salt or to taste

1. Peel the sweet potatoes, and cut into even chunks.

2. Place the sweet potatoes in a large saucepan, and cover them with cold water.

3. Bring the sweet potatoes to a boil over high heat. Turn the heat to medium-low, and let the potatoes boil gently until they are fork tender and very soft.

4. Drain the sweet potatoes, and add them back to the saucepan.

5. Add the butter and coconut milk or heavy cream to the pan, and mix together until the butter is melted.

6. Using a handheld immersion blender or a food processor, process the potato mixture until smooth.

7. Add the nutmeg, and mix well.

8. Season to taste with sea salt.

9. Place the blended sauce back into the saucepan, and heat over medium-low heat. Whisk constantly as it simmers for 3-5 minutes.

10. Remove the pan from the heat, and use the sauce as needed or store in an airtight container in the refrigerator up to 4 days.

PRIMI
PIATTI

*First Courses,
Sauces,
Side Dishes
& Soups*

Basic Tomato Sauce

salsa di pomodoro

Prep Time: 40 minutes   Cook Time: 30 minutes   Yield: Approximately 3 cups

Every recipe must start with a good base, and this basic tomato sauce is an essential ingredient to several delicious recipes in this book. Chef Davide at Vineria Ristorante Eno makes this sauce fresh every day to complement several of his recipes, and I followed suit. You'll find this sauce used in the Eggplant Parmesan (page 136), Mussels & Clams Soup (page 144), and more!

3 pounds Roma tomatoes

2 tablespoons lard, butter, or ghee

2 garlic cloves, halved

I small white onion, finely minced

Sea salt to taste

½ cup fresh basil leaves, diced

I tablespoon fresh oregano, minced

1. In a large pot, add the tomatoes, and cover them with water.

2. Bring the water to a boil over high heat, and cook until the skins begin to peel off.

3. Drain the tomatoes, and let them sit until they are cool enough to handle.

4. When the tomatoes are cool, gently remove the peels, and set them aside.

5. In the same large pot, heat the lard, butter, or ghee over medium heat, and sauté the garlic cloves and onion until the onion is translucent. Turn the heat to low.

6. Run the tomatoes through a food mill back into the large pan with the onion and garlic, leaving behind the seeds.

7. Season with sea salt, and turn the heat back up just a bit. Bring the pot to a simmer, and cook, stirring occasionally, for 20 minutes.

8. Add the fresh basil and oregano, taste, and add more seasoning, if necessary.

9. Serve over zucchini or spaghetti squash noodles.

PRIMI
PIATTI

*First Courses,
Sauces,
Side Dishes
& Soups*

Tomato Cream
crema di pomodoro

Prep Time: 15 minutes   Yield: Approximately 2 cups

This fresh and simple sauce is to be served with the Stuffed Squash Blossoms, but it will also work well as a dipping sauce for the Fried Squash Blossoms.

I pound Roma tomatoes, peeled

I garlic clove

¼ cup extra virgin olive oil

2 tablespoons heavy cream or full-fat canned coconut milk

½ teaspoon sea salt

1. Put all of the Tomato Cream ingredients into a food processor, blender or Vitamix and blend until completely smooth.

2. Serve as a sauce for the Stuffed Squash Blossoms (page 80) or the Fried Squash Blossoms (page 82), or serve as a sauce for any protein of your choice.

PRIMI
PIATTI

*First Courses,
Sauces,
Side Dishes
& Soups*

Red Bell Pepper Sauce

salsa di peperoni rossi

Prep Time: 10 minutes Cook Time: 15-20 minutes
Yield: Approximately 1 cup sauce

This sauce is so easy and tantalizing. Chef Clelia at Lucitta in Sardinia made it for us to accompany her Stuffed Calamari (you'll find my take on this recipe on page 236), and I made my own version of the sauce that I know you'll love. Use this sauce on any protein that you see fit, and you won't be disappointed!

2 red bell peppers

3 tablespoons extra virgin olive oil

1 garlic clove

1 teaspoon sea salt

1. Preheat your oven to 450°F.

2. Line a baking sheet with foil, and place the whole red peppers on the foil. Roast them in the oven for 15-20 minutes or until the skins start to blacken and bubble.

3. Remove the peppers from the oven, and let them cool until you are able to handle them.

4. Remove the skins and seeds from the peppers, and discard them.

5. Place the roasted pepper flesh into a food processor along with the extra virgin olive oil, garlic, and sea salt. Process until completely smooth.

Pesto

pesto

PRIMI
PIATTI

*First Courses,
Sauces,
Side Dishes
& Soups*

Prep Time: 5 minutes   Yield: 1½ cups pesto

Another staple found in several recipes within this book, this Pesto is awesome with eggs or as a condiment on any meat or seafood. For all of the pesto recipes, you may add ½ cup grated Parmesan cheese to the ingredients if you desire.

½ cup toasted pine nuts

1 garlic clove

1 cup extra virgin olive oil

2 cups basil leaves

1 teaspoon sea salt

1.

Place all ingredients in a food processor, and blend together until smooth. Use within 2-3 days if stored in the refrigerator or freeze up to 3 months.

PRIMI
PIATTI
*First Courses,
Sauces,
Side Dishes
& Soups*

Creamy Sun-Dried Tomato Pesto

pesto cremoso ai pomodori secchi

Prep Time: 10 minutes   Yield: Approximately 1½ - 2 cups

¼ cup toasted pine nuts

½ cup sun-dried tomatoes, packed in olive oil, julienne-sliced

½ cup extra virgin olive oil

½ cup Italian parsley

½ cup full-fat canned coconut milk or heavy cream

Sea salt to taste

1.

Add all ingredients to a food processor or Vitamix, and blend until smooth. Store as you would the Pesto.

Sun-Dried Tomato Pesto

pesto con pomodori secchi

Prep Time: 10 minutes   Yield: Approximately 1¼ cups

PRIMI
PIATTI

*First Courses,
Sauces,
Side Dishes
& Soups*

¼ cup toasted pine nuts

½ cup sun-dried tomatoes, packed in olive oil, julienne-sliced

½ cup extra virgin olive oil

½ cup Italian parsley

Sea salt to taste

1.

Add all ingredients to a food processor or Vitamix, and blend until smooth. Store as you would the Pesto.

PRIMI
PIATTI

*First Courses,
Sauces,
Side Dishes
& Soups*

Gnocchi

gnocchi

*Prep Time: **1 hour** Cook Time: **3 minutes** Serves: **5-6***

I made gluten-free gnocchi with Gabriella while cooking at Big Carlo's cooking school in beautiful Bologna. It was made with rice flour, so I was determined to come home and make a completely grain-free version using sweet potatoes. With several attempts and through trial and error, I finally came up with a gnocchi recipe that I felt was good enough to share with all of you. This is a time-consuming adventure, so plan accordingly before you tackle it. Nevertheless, it's loads of fun to make, and I recommend getting the whole family involved! Serve it with Butter & Gold Sauce (page 188), Garlic Sauce (page 190), or Classic Bolognese (page 184). Delicious!

1 pound white sweet potatoes (usually 1 large sweet potato)

1 cup arrowroot flour, plus extra to flour your rolling surface

1 egg

1½ teaspoons sea salt

½ teaspoon nutmeg

2 cups almond flour (I recommend Bob's Red Mill or another finely ground almond flour)

1. Preheat oven to 400°F.

2. Bake the sweet potatoes for 35-40 minutes or until fork tender.

3. Scoop the sweet potatoes from the skins, and then place the sweet potatoes in the freezer for 10 minutes to cool.

4. Once the potatoes are cool, either run them through a potato ricer or mash them with a potato masher. Next, mix the egg, salt, and nutmeg with the sweet potatoes.

5. In a separate bowl, mix the almond flour and arrowroot flour together. Add this mixture, ½ cup at a time, to the sweet potatoes, mixing well until it creates a thick dough.

6. Place a large soup pot filled a little more than halfway with water on the stove over high heat and bring to a boil. While you are waiting for the water to boil, assemble your gnocchi.

7. Use a little more arrowroot flour to lightly flour a flat, even surface. Using a handful of dough at a time, roll the pieces of dough out with your hands into thin rope-like pieces that are about ½-inch thick.

8. Use a knife or pastry cutter to cut the ropes of dough into ½-inch long pieces.

9. Drop the gnocchi a few handfuls at a time into the boiling water.

10. When the gnocchi rise to the top, wait another 30-60 seconds and gently remove with a slotted spoon.

11. At this point you can either spoon your sauce of choice over the cooked gnocchi or quickly sauté the cooked gnocchi in a pan with the sauce of your choice. I recommend the Garlic Sauce (page 190), Butter & Gold (page 188), or the Classic Bolognese (page 184) for your gnocchi.

PRIMI
PIATTI

*First Courses,
Sauces,
Side Dishes
& Soups*

Zucchini & Prosciutto Sauce
sugo di zucchine e prosciutto

Prep Time: 30 minutes   Cook Time: 10-15 minutes   Serves: 5-6

This is one of the first recipes that I made with Big Carlo at his cooking school in Bologna, and again, the fresh ingredients are what make this dish so special. Make sure you also use fresh herbs to complement the zucchini and prosciutto. Enjoy the sauce over any vegetable noodle of your choice. It's delicious as the first course of any meal.

2 tablespoons lard, butter, or ghee

1 small yellow onion, diced

2 garlic cloves, halved

5 zucchini (medium-sized), halved and diced into even pieces

6 ounces prosciutto di parma, diced

1 tablespoon fresh thyme leaves

½ cup Italian parsley, minced

2 tablespoons extra virgin olive oil

Salt and pepper to taste

Spaghetti Squash or Sweet Potato Noodles (page 124)

1. In a large skillet, heat the lard, butter, or ghee over medium heat.

2. Add the onion and garlic, and sauté until the onion starts to caramelize.

3. Add the zucchini and prosciutto, and sauté with the onion and garlic for another 4-7 minutes or until the zucchini is tender.

4. Add the thyme leaves, Italian parsley, extra virgin olive oil, salt and pepper, and stir together.

5. Remove the skillet from the heat, and serve the sauce over the "noodles" of your choice or as a side dish to meat.

PRIMI
PIATTI

First Courses,
Sauces,
Side Dishes
& Soups

Red Clam Sauce

sugo alle vongole rosse

Prep Time: 25 minutes   Cook Time: 10 minutes   Serves: 3-4

This is a classic red clam sauce using beautiful little neck clams as the centerpiece. I love the combination of butter or ghee and olive oil along with the subtle spiciness of the red pepper flakes. Be sure to garnish the dish with fresh Italian parsley!

2 tablespoons butter or ghee

2 garlic cloves, minced

½ cup white wine

¼ cup extra virgin olive oil

½ cup tomato sauce

Pinch red pepper flakes

2 tablespoons Italian parsley, minced

1 pound fresh clams* (if available) and 2 6½-ounce cans canned clams, drained

Zucchini Noodles (page 124)

1. In a medium-sized saucepan, heat the butter or ghee over medium heat.

2. Add the garlic, and sauté just until fragrant.

3. Add the white wine, and bring it to a simmer.

4. Cook the wine for 4-5 minutes, stirring occasionally.

5. Add the extra virgin olive oil, tomato sauce, red chili flakes, Italian parsley, and the fresh clams.

6. Mix well, stirring occasionally. Bring the sauce to a simmer, cover and cook for 5-7 minutes or until all the clams are open. (Fresh clams are done as soon as the shells open wide.)

7. Add the drained canned clams, and stir just until warm, about 1 minute.

8. Remove the sauce from the heat, and serve over the Zucchini Noodles.

*Typically this recipe calls for both fresh and canned clams. If fresh clams are not available, the amount of canned claims called for will be plenty for this dish.

PRIMI
PIATTI

*First Courses,
Sauces,
Side Dishes
& Soups*

White Clam Sauce
sugo alle vongole bianche

Prep Time: 15 minutes   Cook Time: 10 minutes   Serves: 3-4

No need to forgo the white clam sauce if you are steering clear of all dairy products. Simply use coconut milk instead! The lovely white wine and olive oil bring out the flavors in this dish—it's absolutely divine.

¼ *cup butter or ghee*

2 *garlic cloves, minced*

½ *cup dry white wine*

¼ *cup extra virgin olive oil*

2 *tablespoons Italian parsley, minced*

½ *cup full-fat canned coconut milk or heavy cream*

1 *pound fresh clams* (if available) and 2 6½-ounce cans clams, drained*

Zucchini Noodles (page 124)

1. In a medium-sized saucepan, heat the butter or ghee over medium heat.

2. Add the garlic, and sauté just until fragrant.

3. Add the white wine, and bring it to a simmer.

4. Cook the wine for 4-5 minutes, stirring occasionally.

5. Add the extra virgin olive oil, Italian parsley, coconut milk or heavy cream, and the fresh clams.

6. Mix well, stirring occasionally. Bring the sauce to a simmer, and cook for 5-7 minutes or until all of the clams are open. (Fresh clams are done as soon as the shells are open wide.)

7. Add the drained canned clams, stir and cook until warm, about 1 minute.

8. Remove the sauce from the heat, and serve it over the Zucchini Noodles.

*Typically this recipe calls for both fresh and canned clams. If fresh clams are not available, the amount of canned claims called for will be plenty for this dish.

PRIMI
PIATTI
*First Courses,
Sauces,
Side Dishes
& Soups*

Puttanesca Sauce
sugo alla puttanesca

Another classic, this delicious sauce is great on veggie noodles but also goes well over eggs or paired with grilled chicken. Try it over seafood, too. Simply grill some fresh fish, and spoon this sauce on top right before it's served. Versatile and full of flavor, this is a go-to sauce that the whole family will enjoy!

2 tablespoons lard, butter, or ghee

1 yellow onion, finely diced

3 garlic cloves, minced

1 28-ounce can San Marzano tomatoes

1 tablespoon anchovy fillets, finely minced

2 tablespoons capers

1 6-ounce can whole black olives

½ teaspoon red pepper flakes

2-3 tablespoons extra virgin olive oil

½ cup fresh Italian parsley, chopped

Sea salt and black pepper to taste

Vegetable noodles of your choice (page 124)

1. In a large saucepan, heat the lard, butter, or ghee over medium-high heat, and sauté the onion until translucent.

2. Add the garlic, and sauté just until fragrant.

3. Add the tomatoes, and bring them to a simmer, breaking down the whole tomatoes with a spoon.

4. Add the anchovies and capers, mix well, and simmer for 5-10 min.

5. Add the olives, red pepper flakes, extra virgin olive oil, Italian parsley, and salt and pepper to taste.

6. Simmer for another 5-10 minutes, and serve over the vegetable noodles of your choice or over any meat such as meatballs, steak, or chicken.

PRIMI
PIATTI

First Courses,
Sauces,
Side Dishes
& Soups

Spicy Sausage Spaghetti

spaghetti alla salsiccia piccante

Prep Time: 30 minutes   Cook Time: 20 minutes   Serves: 5

I love making a dish with veggies and meat combined together, and with this scrumptious sauce, you can turn it into a meal or a first course depending on your mood. The broccolini adds color and crunch, and if you don't like it spicy, you can use mild Italian sausage instead of the suggested spicy sausage. Enjoy!

2 pounds spicy Italian sausage, casings removed

1 yellow onion, diced

3-4 cups broccolini, chopped

2 garlic cloves, diced

½ cup (or more to taste) Sun-Dried Tomato Pesto (page 169)

Spaghetti Squash or Sweet Potato Noodles (page 124)

1. Heat a large skillet over medium heat, and crumble in the spicy sausage. Cook until the sausage is browned and almost cooked all the way through.

2. Add the onion, and cook until the sausage is fully cooked and the onion is translucent.

3. Add the broccolini, garlic, and Sun-Dried Tomato Pesto, and cook for another 5-8 minutes, stirring often or until the broccolini is tender.

4. Serve over Spaghetti Squash or Sweet Potato Noodles.

PRIMI
PIATTI

First Courses,
Sauces,
Side Dishes
& Soups

Sarah's Spaghetti Carbonara
spaghetti alla carbonara

Prep Time: 20 minutes   Cook Time: 15 minutes   Serves: 3-4

This is my spin on the classic spaghetti carbonara, which has received rave reviews! Creamy, savory, and with just a little kick, this one is a crowd-pleaser. Make this for your family members who miss pasta. Serve it over sweet potato noodles, and you'll have some very happy former pasta lovers!

2 tablespoons lard, butter, or ghee

12 ounces pancetta or bacon, diced

1 red bell pepper, diced

2 cups mushrooms, diced

¼ cup Italian parsley, diced

¼ cup full-fat canned coconut milk or heavy cream

1 teaspoon red pepper flakes (or to taste)

Sea salt and pepper to taste

Spaghetti Squash or Sweet Potato Noodles (page 124)

1. In a large skillet, heat the lard, butter, or ghee over medium heat.

2. Add the pancetta, and cook until it starts to brown.

3. Add the bell pepper and mushrooms, and cook until the bell pepper is tender, stirring often.

4. Add the Italian parsley, coconut milk, and red pepper flakes, and bring the mixture to a simmer. Let it cook, stirring often, for another 3-4 minutes.

5. Season to taste with salt and pepper, and serve it over either Spaghetti Squash or Sweet Potato Noodles.

PRIMI
PIATTI

*First Courses,
Sauces,
Side Dishes
& Soups*

Classic Bolognese
ragù alla bolognese

Prep Time: 30 minutes Cook Time: 1 hour Serves: 5-6

Watching Big Carlo make this classic sauce was like watching magic happen. It's about love, time, and quality ingredients, and this sauce is a combination of all of those things. Make this on a day when you want to linger in the kitchen, enjoy a glass of wine, and watch your sauce simmer and turn into an amazing yet simple Classic Bolognese. Thank you, Big Carlo, for sharing your warmth, passion, and love for real Italian cooking.

4 carrots

4 celery stalks

1 small yellow onion

1 tablespoon lard

1 pound ground bacon (ask your butcher to grind it for you or you can use ground pork)

2 pounds ground beef

½ cup red wine

1 28-ounce can San Marzano whole tomatoes with sauce

1 cup heavy cream or ½ cup full-fat canned coconut milk

Salt to taste

Spaghetti Squash or Zucchini Noodles (page 124)

1. Cut the carrots, celery, and onion into large chunks, and place them into a food processor. Process until minced.

2. In a large skillet, melt the lard over medium heat.

3. Add the minced veggies to the lard, and cook for 3 minutes.

4. Add the ground bacon or pork, and cook for 3 minutes.

5. Add the ground beef, and cook until the moisture is almost gone from the pan.

6. Add the red wine, and cook for 10 minutes.

7. Add the tomatoes, breaking them down with a spoon, and bring the liquid to a simmer. Cook for another 20-30 minutes, stirring occasionally.

8. Add the heavy cream or coconut milk, and mix well. Bring to a simmer again for 5-10 minutes.

9. Taste, and season with salt as desired.

10. Serve over Spaghetti Squash or Zucchini Noodles.

PRIMI
PIATTI

First Courses,
Sauces,
Side Dishes
& Soups

Baked "Ziti"
ziti al forno

Prep Time: 45 minutes   Cook Time: 1 hour   Serves: 5-6

This treasured classic is found throughout Italy. The preparation and technique vary by region, but ultimately it's a baked pasta dish with a rich tomato sauce. I re-created this classic using butternut squash rather than pasta and added Italian sausage for a meatier version. My friends and family members who have eaten this dish have claimed it to be one of the best recipes in the book!

1 pound butternut squash peeled and cut into ¼-inch thick and approximately 2-inch long pieces, just make sure they are all even and about the size of a piece of ziti pasta

1 tablespoon tallow or lard

1 pound mild Italian sausage, casings removed

½ pound hot Italian sausage, casings removed (or use all mild if you do not want any spice)

1 small yellow onion, diced

3-4 tablespoons garlic cloves, minced

1 28-ounce can San Marzano whole tomatoes

¼ cup coconut milk or heavy cream

1 tablespoon fresh oregano, chopped

1 teaspoon fresh thyme, chopped

2 tablespoons fresh basil, chopped

Sea salt and black pepper to taste

OPTIONAL

Parmesan and sliced mozzarella cheese

1. Preheat oven to 350°F.

2. In a 9" X 13" baking dish, evenly spread the cut butternut squash.

3. In a large soup pot or large deep skillet heat the tallow or lard over medium heat and crumble in the mild and spicy sausage; add the onion and cook together until the sausage is browned.

4. Add the garlic and cook for another minute or two.

5. Add the tomatoes and bring to a simmer, breaking up the tomatoes with your spoon.

6. Add the coconut milk or heavy cream, oregano, thyme, and basil, and season to taste with salt and pepper.

7. Stir well and bring to a simmer for another 5-7 minutes.

8. Pour the sauce evenly over the butternut squash.

9. Bake uncovered for 40-45 minutes or until the squash is fork tender.

10. If desired sprinkle a layer of Parmesan and then a layer of mozzarella on top of the dish and bake for an additional 10 minutes or until the cheese is melted.

PRIMI
PIATTI

First Courses,
Sauces,
Side Dishes
& Soups

Butter & Gold

burro e oro

Prep Time: 10 minutes   Cook Time: 15 minutes
Yield: Approximately 4 cups of sauce

Burro e Oro translates to Butter & Gold, a perfect description for this silky, creamy, delicious sauce. I could eat this sauce with a spoon like soup (try it; I know you'll agree), but I love it even more poured over my Gnocchi (page 170). I learned to make this sauce while cooking with Big Carlo in Bologna, and I hope you enjoy my take on this Italian classic!

7 tablespoons butter or ghee

2 garlic cloves, minced

2½ cups tomato sauce

1 cup full-fat canned coconut milk or heavy cream

Sea salt to taste

2 tablespoons fresh basil, minced

1. In a large sauté pan, melt the butter or ghee over medium heat.

2. Add the garlic, and sauté for 3-4 minutes.

3. Add the tomato sauce, and whisk together with the butter until blended. Bring it to a simmer.

4. In a small separate saucepan, heat the coconut milk or heavy cream over medium-high heat just until it's warm.

5. Add the warm coconut milk or cream to the tomato and butter half at a time, and whisk well.

6. Season to taste with sea salt, add the basil, and let it simmer for another 5-7 minutes.

7. Serve over the Gnocchi (page 170) or vegetable noodles of your choice (page 124).

PRIMI
PIATTI
First Courses,
Sauces,
Side Dishes
& Soups

Garlic Sauce
sugo all'aglio

Prep Time: 10 minutes   Cook Time: 5 minutes   Yield: ¾ cup sauce

Luciana, one of Big Carlo's teachers at his cooking school, introduced me to this garlic sauce. Her version is simply an entire head of garlic finely minced and mixed with high quality extra virgin olive oil and Parmesan cheese. She served it to us over gluten-free gnocchi. As she made the sauce, she explained that it's so powerful that when you eat it, you must be careful because if someone walks into the room and smells that you have eaten all of this garlic, "Boom, they fall on the floor dead!" She wasn't kidding. Now, I love garlic like crazy, but straight raw garlic and olive oil served in abundance is even too much for me. So, I toned it down a bit by first cooking the garlic in butter or ghee and then adding in the olive oil. It's delicious and mellower than the original version. However, if you happen to have a problem with vampires or want to risk your relationships, go for Luciana's version instead of mine!

2 tablespoons butter or ghee

5 garlic cloves, minced

½ cup extra virgin olive oil

Sea salt to taste

1. In a medium sized skillet, heat the butter over medium heat.

2. Add the garlic, and sauté for 4-5 minutes or until it just starts to brown.

3. Turn the heat off, add the extra virgin olive oil, and whisk together with the butter and garlic.

4. Season with a bit of sea salt, and serve the sauce over Gnocchi (page 170) or over grilled steak. Use all of the sauce immediately, do not store for later use. Discard any leftover or unused sauce.

PRIMI
PIATTI

*First Courses,
Sauces,
Side Dishes
& Soups*

Calamari & Spinach Sauce

sugo con calamari e spinaci

Prep Time: 30 minutes   Cook Time: 15 minutes   Serves: 4-5

This was another classic recipe that I learned while cooking with Big Carlo in Bologna. I watched Carlo's sister cook this recipe with precision, just as her family had for generations. This is my own twist, and it's so full of flavor–light, bright, and satisfying. If you are unable to find fresh calamari, feel free to use shrimp or the fish of your choice. You can even use chicken.

1 tablespoon lard, butter, or ghee

1 garlic clove, cut in half

4 ounces prosciutto, diced

¼ cup white wine

1 pound calamari, cleaned and cut into rings (also use the tentacles)

1 cup cherry tomatoes, cut in half

6 ounces fresh spinach leaves

3 tablespoons extra virgin olive oil

¼ cup chives, finely diced

¼ cup basil, finely diced

1-2 teaspoons lemon juice

Sea salt and black pepper to taste

Spaghetti Squash or Zucchini Noodles 124)

1. In a large sauté pan, heat the lard, butter, or ghee over medium heat.

2. Add the garlic, and sauté for 2-3 minutes.

3. Add the prosciutto, and sauté for another 2-3 minutes.

4. Add the white wine, and reduce down, stirring often, for 1-2 minutes.

5. Add the calamari and tomato halves, and sauté for 4-5 minutes.

6. Add the spinach leaves, and sauté just until the leaves are wilted.

7. Remove the pan from the heat, and stir in the extra virgin olive oil, chives, basil, and lemon juice. Season to taste with salt and pepper.

8. Serve the sauce over Spaghetti Squash or Zucchini Noodles.

Note: If you opt to clean the calamari yourself instead of buying pre-cleaned, the prep time increases from 30 minutes to 1 hour.

PRIMI
PIATTI

First Courses,
Sauces,
Side Dishes
& Soups

Sausage and Fennel Sauce
sugo con salsiccia e finocchi

Prep Time: 30 minutes   Cook Time: 30 minutes   Serves: 5

Fragrant fennel makes this recipe very special, as does Chef Davide's inspired Basic Tomato Sauce. I enjoy this dish served over the Sweet Potato Noodles, and my boys ask for this meal often. It's also easy to double the recipe if you want to serve a crowd. Note: If don't already have the Basic Tomato Sauce prepared, the preparation and cook time will increase slightly.

2 cups Basic Tomato Sauce (page 162)

2 pounds mild Italian pork sausage, casings removed

2 large fennel bulbs, quartered and diced (about 2½ cups)

3 garlic cloves, minced

1 teaspoon red pepper flakes, more or less to taste

1 tablespoon lard, butter, or ghee

Spaghetti Squash, Sweet Potato, or Zucchini Noodles (page 124)

1. Make the Basic Tomato Sauce.

2. In a large sauté pan, add the lard, butter, or ghee and crumble the sausage, and brown it over medium heat.

3. Add the diced fennel, and sauté with the sausage until the fennel is tender, approximately 7-8 minutes.

4. Add the garlic, and sauté another 2-3 minutes.

5. Add the Tomato Sauce and the red pepper flakes, and mix well.

6. Bring the sauce to a simmer for 4-5 minutes, stirring occasionally.

7. Serve the sauce over the vegetable noodles of your choice.

PRIMI
PIATTI

*First Courses,
Sauces,
Side Dishes
& Soups*

Mushroom "Risotto"

risotto ai funghi

Prep Time: 15 minutes   Cook Time: 30 minutes   Serves: 5-6

I will never forget my first trip with Big Carlo to the outdoor market in Bologna, where we met the farmers, butchers, and fishmongers. Together, Carlo and I picked out the most beautiful porcini mushrooms I have ever seen, and Carlo taught me how to make risotto. This is my version of Carlo's risotto, made daringly with cauliflower instead of rice! I was amazed, inspired, and thrilled with how this turned out, and I'm confident you will enjoy it too.

1 small head cauliflower (approximately 4 cups once processed)

3 tablespoons butter, ghee, or lard

3 garlic cloves, halved

3-4 cups mushrooms, sliced

¼ cup white wine

1 cup Chicken Broth (page 141)

½ cup heavy cream or coconut milk

2 tablespoons Italian parsley, minced + more for garnish, if desired

Salt and pepper to taste

Extra virgin olive oil

1. Cut the head of the cauliflower into florets, place them in a food processor, and pulse until the cauliflower is in small pieces similar to the consistency and size of rice.

2. In a large sauté pan or skillet, heat the butter, ghee, or lard over medium heat.

3. Add the garlic and mushrooms, and sauté for 3-5 minutes.

4. Turn the heat to medium-high, and add the white wine. Cook, stirring often, for another 3-4 minutes.

5. Add the cauliflower, and stir well.

6. Add the Chicken Broth and heavy cream or coconut milk, and stir.

7. Once the cauliflower starts to simmer, turn the heat to medium-low, and cook for another 7-10 minutes.

8. Add the Italian parsley, mix well, and season to taste with salt and pepper.

9. Garnish with more minced Italian parsley, if desired, and a drizzle of extra virgin olive oil.

PRIMI
PIATTI
*First Courses,
Sauces,
Side Dishes
& Soups*

"Risotto" alla Milanese

Prep Time: 40 minutes   Cook Time: 1.5 hours   Serves: 5-6

I learned from Anna Maria and Anna in Rome how to make Ossobuco and "Risotto" alla Milanese–the bone marrow is the secret! Made with cauliflower instead of rice, my version of "Risotto" alla Milanese is truly out of this world and does not disappoint, even without the rice. Give yourself some time to make this recipe, and make sure you pair it with the Ossobuco (page 222) because you truly cannot make one without the other.

1 head cauliflower (approximately 4 cups once processed)

2 pounds beef marrowbones

1-2 cups Beef Broth (page 140)

2 tablespoons tallow, butter, or ghee

½ yellow onion, finely diced

1 teaspoon saffron threads

¼ cup white wine

¼ cup Italian parsley, finely diced

Sea salt and black pepper to taste

1. Cut the head of the cauliflower into florets, place them in a food processor, and pulse until the cauliflower is in small pieces similar to the consistency and size of rice. Set aside.

2. Preheat your oven to 400°F.

3. Line a baking sheet with foil, and place the marrowbones evenly on the baking sheet.

4. Bake in the oven for 45 minutes.

5. Once the bones are cool enough to handle, scoop out the roasted bone marrow, finely mince it, and set it aside.

6. Meanwhile, in a saucepan, heat the Beef Broth over medium-high heat until it simmers. Turn the heat to low, and keep the broth warm.

7. In a large sauté pan, add the tallow, butter, or ghee and heat it over medium heat. Add the onion, and sauté it until it is browned.

8. Add the beef marrow, and sauté for 1-2 minutes.

9. Add the processed cauliflower, and mix well.

10. In a small bowl, add the saffron threads, and pour about ¼ of the hot beef broth over the saffron. Set the bowl aside.

11. Meanwhile, cook the cauliflower with the onion and beef marrow for 7-10 minutes, stirring often.

12. Add the white wine to the pan, and cook for another 3-5 minutes.

13. Add the saffron-infused beef broth, and mix well.

14. Add another 1½ cups of the Beef Broth to the pan, and bring it to a simmer with the cauliflower.

15. Stir in the Italian parsley, and season to taste with salt and pepper. Serve it with the Ossobuco (page 222).

SECONDI PIATTI

Main Dishes

Lasagna

Prep Time: 1 hour   Cook Time: 1.5 hours   Serves: 6-7

I. Love. Lasagna. I do not miss pasta all that much, but I do miss the comfort of a delicious deep-dish casserole. Although I have another lasagna recipe in **Everyday Paleo** *that is great, this one takes the cake. Many traditional Italian lasagna recipes call for Béchamel sauce, which is made with flour and cream, and once I mastered a Paleo version of this sauce, I knew my lasagna would be complete. I enjoy the portobello mushrooms as a lasagna noodle replacement. They provide great texture, as well as plenty of flavor. Have fun with this one, and make sure you have friends and family with you because this is definitely a meal to share with the ones you love.*

2 tablespoons lard, tallow, butter, or ghee

I cup celery, diced

I cup carrots, diced

I cup yellow onion, diced

2 pounds ground beef

I pound ground pork

¼ cup white wine

3 garlic cloves, minced

I 28-ounce can crushed tomatoes

I 6-ounce can tomato paste

3 teaspoons dried oregano

2 tablespoons dried basil

Sea salt and black pepper to taste

12 ounces portobello mushrooms, ribs removed and thinly sliced or 12 ounces eggplant thinly sliced with a mandoline

3 cups Béchamel Sauce (page 160)

1. Make the Béchamel Sauce.

2. Preheat your oven to 350°F.

3. In a large skillet, heat the lard, butter, or ghee over medium heat.

4. Add the celery, carrots, and onion, and sauté for 5 minutes.

5. Add the ground beef and ground pork, and continue to cook until the meat is browned.

6. Add the white wine, garlic, crushed tomatoes, tomato paste, oregano, and basil, and mix well.

7. Bring the mixture to a simmer over medium-low heat for 20-30 minutes, stirring occasionally.

8. Season the sauce to taste with sea salt and black pepper.

9. In a 9" X 13" baking dish or deep-dish lasagna pan, place a layer of the thinly sliced portobello mushrooms. Then, ladle on a layer of meat sauce, another layer of mushrooms, a layer of Béchamel Sauce, and another layer of meat sauce. Continue to alternate the layers until the meat sauce is gone. End with a final layer of the Béchamel Sauce.

10. Bake uncovered in the oven for 45 minutes.

11. Remove the lasagna from the oven, and let it sit for 20 minutes. Top with any remaining Béchamel Sauce before cutting and serving.

Mushroom Meatballs
with Easy Tomato Sauce
polpette di funghi in salsa al pomodoro

Prep Time: 45 minutes   Cook Time: 30 minutes   Serves: 5-6

Succulent meatballs swimming in a sea of easy-to-make tomato sauce! This is comfort food at its finest. Frying the meatballs first will seal in the flavors, and the brightness of the fresh basil at the end ties it all together.

MEATBALLS

1 pound mushrooms of your choice, finely diced

1 pound ground beef

2 garlic cloves, minced

½ cup Italian parsley, finely minced

2 egg yolks

2 teaspoons salt

1 teaspoon black pepper

1-2 tablespoons lard, butter, or ghee for frying the meatballs

SAUCE

1 28-ounce can Marzano tomatoes

3 tablespoons extra virgin olive oil

1 cup fresh basil, chopped

Sea salt and black pepper to taste

1. In a large mixing bowl, use your hands to combine the mushrooms, beef, garlic, Italian parsley, egg yolks, salt, and pepper.

2. Shape the meat mixture into meatballs that are slightly larger than a golf ball.

3. In a large sauté pan, heat the lard, butter, or ghee over medium-high heat. Add the meatballs to the hot pan, and brown them on all sides.

4. Remove the browned meatballs from the pan, and set them aside.

5. Make the sauce by adding the tomatoes, olive oil, basil, and salt and pepper to taste to the same pan used for the meatballs. Cook over medium heat, and bring the sauce to a simmer, stirring occasionally.

6. Add the meatballs to the simmering sauce, cover, and simmer over low heat for 15-20 minutes or until the meatballs are cooked all the way through.

Meatballs & Spinach
with Béchamel Sauce

polpette di spinaci e besciamella

Prep Time: 45 minutes   Cook Time: 15 minutes   Serves: 6

It isn't hard to find an excuse to use Béchamel Sauce. This recipe is a home run with the duo of savory meatballs and the sweetness of the creamy sauce. I like these paired with the Radicchio with Pancetta Dressing (page 106) for a delicious weeknight family meal.

Béchamel Sauce (page 160)

2 pounds ground beef

2 egg yolks

2 cups spinach, finely chopped

4 garlic cloves, minced

2 tablespoons fresh sage, minced

2 teaspoons sea salt

1 teaspoon black pepper

4-6 tablespoons lard, butter, or ghee for frying

1. Make the Béchamel Sauce, and cover it to keep it warm while you prepare the meatballs.

2. In a large bowl, use your hands to mix together the beef, egg yolks, spinach, garlic, sage, salt, and pepper.

3. Form the meat mixture into meatballs that are slightly larger than a golf ball.

4. In a large skillet, heat the lard, butter, or ghee over medium heat. Add the meatballs, and cook until all sides are evenly browned.

5. Cover the meatballs, turn the heat to low, and let them cook covered for another 7-10 minutes or until they are done all the way through.

6. Serve with the Béchamel Sauce.

Note: The 45 minute prep includes the time it takes to make the Béchamel Sauce.

Lamb with Aromatic Herbs

agnello alle erbette aromatiche

Prep Time: 30 minutes   Cook Time: 15 minutes   Serves: 3-5

This recipe is the magic of Chef Samuele. In fact, we devoured these lamb chops as soon as they left the pan! As with anything else, I can never leave "good enough" alone, so I did add my own twist to the dish by searing the lamb chops first in lard. I also added the olive oil at the end rather than poaching the lamb in the liquid. If you are a lamb lover, I guarantee you'll be going back to this recipe time and time again.

1 rack of lamb, Frenched and cut into chops (usually between 7-8 ribs)

3 tablespoons lard, butter, or ghee

3 garlic cloves, minced

1 cup white wine

2 tablespoons fresh rosemary, minced

2 tablespoons fresh sage, minced

¾ cup extra virgin olive oil

Sea salt to taste

1. Season the lamb chops on both sides with sea salt and set them aside.

2. In a large skillet, heat the lard, butter, or ghee over medium-high heat.

3. Once the fat is hot, add the seasoned lamb chops, and brown them on each side for 3-4 minutes.

4. Remove the chops from the pan, and set them aside.

5. Add the garlic to the hot pan, and sauté it for 1-2 minutes.

6. Add the wine to the hot pan with the garlic to deglaze the pan, and whisk well. Let it simmer for 5-7 minutes, letting the wine reduce down just a bit.

7. Add the rosemary, sage, and extra virgin olive oil to the pan, and stir just until warm.

8. Add the lamb chops back to the sauce, and make sure the lamb is coated with the sauce.

9. Bring the chops to a simmer over medium heat for another 3-4 minutes.

10. Serve the lamb topped with the herb sauce, and season it with more sea salt, if desired.

Lamb with Lemon & Eggs

agnello con uova e limone

Prep Time: 20 minutes   Cook Time: 15-20 minutes   Serves: 4-5

I know that a recipe for lamb with lemon and eggs sounds a little odd, but trust me, it's so darn good! Chef Andrea at Casa Marmida made this dish for us, and I was amazed at how the eggs made the sauce creamy at the end and not "eggy"! This is my version of his awesome recipe. The fresh herbs, as always, bring brightness and flavor to this unique and tantalizing meal.

2-3 tablespoons lard, duck fat, butter, or ghee

2 garlic cloves, cut in half

2 pounds lamb loin chops

¼ cup red wine

½ cup Vegetable Broth (page 138)

1 tablespoon fresh oregano leaves, minced

1 tablespoon Italian parsley, minced

1 egg

Juice from half a lemon

Sea salt to taste

1. In a large sauté pan, heat the lard, duck fat, butter, or ghee over medium-high heat.

2. Add the halved garlic cloves to the oil, and sauté for 1-2 minutes.

3. Sprinkle all sides of the lamb chops with sea salt, and sear them in the oil in the hot pan on both sides until browned.

4. Add the red wine to the hot pan with the lamb chops, and simmer for 1-2 minutes.

5. Add the Vegetable Broth, oregano, and Italian parsley, and bring the mixture to a simmer. Stir to coat the lamb with the herbs.

6. Meanwhile, in a small bowl, whisk the egg together with the lemon juice.

7. While the liquid is hot and simmering, add the whisked lemon juice and egg to the liquid, stirring constantly. Continue stirring for 1-2 minutes.

8. Season with sea salt, and serve the lamb with the sauce.

Steak with Artichokes

bistecca con carciofi

Prep Time: 45 minutes   Cook Time: 15-20 minutes   Serves: 3-4

If you are new to cleaning an artichoke, follow the step-by-step instructions found on page 214. Prior to my trip to Italy, I would only eat artichokes that had been steamed or boiled. I pulled the leaves off, dipped them in butter or ghee, and ate them. My eyes were opened to so many more possibilities during our journey around Italy. I ate artichokes raw, sautéed, steamed, and fried, and loved them every single way I had them! Artichokes are wildly popular in Italy, and when in season, you'll see them served just about everywhere. Sautéing the artichokes with delicious fat and then drowning them in good white wine and homemade Chicken Broth is seriously delectable. I'm so glad that Chef Roberto and Chef Andrea showed me this technique served over various proteins. This recipe calls for steak, but feel free to serve these artichokes over any meat of your choice. It's also excellent with lamb!

4 tablespoons lard, butter, or ghee

2 large artichokes, cleaned and thinly sliced (see page 214 for how to clean an artichoke)

2 garlic cloves, cut in half

¼ cup white wine

¼ cup Chicken Broth (page 141)

1 tablespoon fresh thyme leaves, minced

Sea salt and black pepper to taste

3-4 rib eye or t-bone steaks (more or less depending upon how many people you are serving; the artichokes will be enough to top at least 4 steaks)

Basil Oil (page 159)

1. In a large skillet, heat the lard, butter, or ghee over medium-high heat.

2. When the oil is hot, add the sliced artichoke hearts and garlic, and sauté for 5-7 minutes or until the artichokes start to brown.

3. Add the wine, and stir well to deglaze the pan.

4. Let the wine reduce down by half, and add the Chicken Broth, thyme, and salt and pepper to taste.

5. Stir well, and bring the mixture to a simmer. Turn off the heat, and cover the pan to keep the ingredients warm.

6. Meanwhile, season your steaks with sea salt, and grill or pan-fry your meat to your desired doneness.

7. Top each steak with a spoonful of the artichoke heart mixture and a drizzle of Basil Oil.

How to Clean an Artichoke

1. Cut off the stem of the artichoke and remove the tough outer layer of leaves until you reach the lighter colored, tender leaves.

2. Cut the spiny tips off the artichoke.

3. Cut the artichoke in half lengthwise.

4. Use a paring knife to gently scoop out the small feathery leaves that cover the heart and discard.

5. Place the artichoke flat side down and thinly slice the artichoke into strips.

Beef, Lamb, or Mutton Stew

stufato di manzo, agnello o montone

Prep Time: 30 minutes   Cook Time: 1.5 hours   Serves: 5

Sheep stew? Why not? Those were my exact thoughts when Chef Andrea from Casa Marmida informed us what he was making. I love lamb, but mutton has always scared me a bit. I don't know why, but eating a big ol' sheep just doesn't seem very yummy. Well, boy, was I wrong! This stew was out of this world good with saffron and sage, sun-dried tomatoes, homemade Vegetable Broth, and delicious chunks of simmering meat. Although it isn't easy to find mutton at home, it's easy for me to get grass-fed beef in the U.S., and I've made this several times now with beef instead. It's just as delicious.

2 tablespoons lard, butter, or ghee

2 pounds beef, lamb, or mutton stew meat

1 white onion, finely diced

½ cup sun-dried tomatoes, minced

3 garlic cloves, minced

¼ cup water

Sea salt to taste

1 28-ounce can whole tomatoes

1½ cups Vegetable Broth (page 138)

1 big pinch saffron threads

2 large sweet potatoes, cubed

1 tablespoon fresh rosemary, minced

1 tablespoon fresh sage leaves, minced

2 tablespoons extra virgin olive oil

1. In a large soup pot, heat the lard, butter, or ghee over medium-high heat. Add the stew meat to the hot oil, and brown for 4-5 minutes.

2. Remove the meat from the pan with a slotted spoon, and set it aside.

3. Add the onion and sun-dried tomatoes to the same pan, and sauté them together until the onion is translucent.

4. Add the garlic, and sauté just until fragrant, about 1 minute.

5. Add the water, and stir well to deglaze the pan.

6. Add the stew meat back to the pot, season with a bit of sea salt, and add the tomatoes. Turn the heat to medium-low, stir well, and let the stew simmer.

7. Meanwhile, in a separate small saucepan, heat the Vegetable Broth over medium-high heat.

8. When the broth is simmering, add the saffron threads, and simmer for 2-3 minutes.

9. Add the saffron-infused broth to the stew pot, and stir well.

10. Raise the heat on the stew to medium-high, and bring the stew to a simmer.

11. Cover, turn the heat to low, and simmer for 30 minutes, stirring occasionally.

12. Add the sweet potatoes and rosemary, and simmer uncovered for another 30-45 minutes, stirring occasionally, until the meat is fork tender and the potatoes are done.

13. Add the sage, season to taste with sea salt, and right before serving, stir in the extra virgin olive oil.

Beef or Mutton Fillet with
Pomegranate Reduction & Spring Salad

filetto di manzo o montone con riduzione di melagrana e misticanza

Prep Time: 45 minutes   Cook Time: 8-10 minutes   Serves: 4-5

Collectively, our crew decided that this was one of the best things we ate while in Italy— another reminder that fresh, high-quality ingredients are all you need to make food taste great. Maybe it was also the fact that the lettuce was grown right outside the door, or maybe it was because the mutton came from just across the yard from sheep that grazed on open fields of grass. Or maybe it was the fresh pomegranate vinaigrette. Whatever it was, this combination is delectable, and I'm confident that your own creation will take you straight to the bountiful farmland of Sardinia.

MEAT

2 pounds beef or mutton fillets

Sea salt

3 tablespoons lard, butter, or ghee

POMEGRANATE VINAIGRETTE

3 tablespoons pomegranate juice

¼ cup extra virgin olive oil

1 tablespoon lemon juice

1 tablespoon fresh oregano, minced

Sea salt and black pepper to taste

SALAD

8-10 ounces mixed organic greens

1 cup pomegranate seeds

1 cup cherry tomato halves

POMEGRANATE REDUCTION

1 cup pomegranate juice

1. Season the beef or mutton steaks with sea salt.

2. In a large skillet, heat the lard, butter, or ghee over medium high heat.

3. Once the pan is hot, sear the steaks on all sides for 3-4 minutes per side for medium rare.

4. Remove the steaks from the pan, and let them rest while you prepare the remainder of the meal.

5. Make the vinaigrette by whisking the pomegranate juice, extra virgin olive oil, lemon juice, oregano, and salt and pepper to taste. Set the dressing aside.

6. Toss together the organic greens, pomegranate seeds, and cherry tomato halves, and set the salad aside.

7. In a small saucepan, reduce the pomegranate juice over medium-high heat by half, or until it becomes like a syrup, stirring often.

8. Pour the vinaigrette over the salad, and toss to coat.

9. Slice the meat into small pieces, and arrange it on top of the salad.

10. Drizzle the meat with the pomegranate reduction, and serve immediately.

Steak with Savory Onions and Grapes

bistecca con cipolle alla santoreggia e uva

Prep Time: 15 minutes   **Cook Time:** 15-20 minutes   **Yield:** 4-5 steaks

This recipe is inspired by the meal we ate at Vineria Ristorante Eno in Cagliari on the island of Sardinia. After cooking with Chef Davide, our crew stayed for dinner, and this is one of the dishes we ordered. I created my own version back at home, and it's surprising and delicious. The combination of the sweetness from the grapes and the caramelized onion served over juicy grilled steak will make you as happy as it has made my family.

2 tablespoons tallow, lard, butter, or ghee

I medium white onion, halved and thinly sliced

2 garlic cloves, cut in half

I cup red grapes, halved

I tablespoon fresh rosemary, minced

I tablespoon balsamic vinegar

I tablespoon extra virgin olive oil

Sea salt to taste

3-5 sirloin or rib eye steaks, or as many as needed

1. In a large skillet, heat the tallow, butter, or ghee over medium heat.

2. Once the oil is hot, add the onion, and sauté it until it begins to brown.

3. Add the garlic, and sauté it with the onion for another 3-4 minutes.

4. Add the grapes, rosemary, and balsamic vinegar, and sauté for another 3-4 minutes.

5. Remove the skillet from the heat, and add the extra virgin olive oil and sea salt to taste.

6. Cover the skillet to keep the ingredients warm, and set it aside.

7. Meanwhile, season the steaks with sea salt, and grill or pan-fry the meat to your desired doneness.

8. Top each steak with a spoonful of the grilled onions and grapes.

Ossobuco

Prep Time: 45 minutes   Cook Time: 2 hours   Serves: 5

I'm not a huge fan of veal, but this is a true classic Italian meal. While in Rome cooking with Anna Maria and Anna, I knew I had to learn how to make this dish straight from the source. So, now I like veal, as long as it's this particular recipe. The flavors in this dish and the slow cooking process were a game-changer for me. If you are also not a veal fan, you can use regular beef shanks, but otherwise make this as suggested. You will not be disappointed. Of course, you must pair this with the "Risotto" alla Milanese found on page 198.

GREMOLATA

Lemon zest from 2 lemons (2 tablespoons)

6 garlic cloves, minced

⅓ cup fresh Italian parsley, finely diced

4 tablespoons lard, butter, or ghee

3 pounds veal or beef shanks, cut into 2-3-inch pieces

1 large yellow onion, diced

3 large carrots, diced

4 celery stalks, diced

4 garlic cloves, minced

⅓ cup white wine or more as needed

1 14-ounce can tomato sauce or 14 ounces Basic Tomato Sauce (page 162)

1 cup Beef Broth (page 140) or more as needed

Sea salt and black pepper to taste

2 bay leaves

1 large rosemary sprig

5-6 sage leaves

1 teaspoon lemon zest

1. Make the Gremolata by mixing together the lemon zest, garlic, and parsley. Set it aside.

2. In a large stockpot or Dutch oven, melt the lard, butter, or ghee over medium-high heat.

3. Season the veal or beef shanks with salt and pepper, and sear them on all sides until browned. Remove the browned shanks from the pot, and set them aside.

4. To the same hot pan, add the onion, carrots, and celery, and sauté for 4-5 minutes.

5. Add the garlic, and sauté for another 3-4 minutes.

6. Add the white wine and cook, stirring often for 3-4 minutes.

7. Add the tomato sauce and Beef Broth, and bring it to a simmer.

8. Season to taste with salt and pepper.

9. Add the meat back to the sauce, and make sure the shanks are covered with sauce.

10. Add the bay leaves, rosemary, and sage to the pan.

11. Sprinkle lemon zest on top, cover, and cook for 1½ hours, turning the meat occasionally. The meat should be fork tender when done.

12. Serve topped with the Gremolata and accompanied by the "Risotto" alla Milanese (page 198).

Fish Burgers

hamburger di pesce

Prep Time: 45 minutes   Cook Time: 7-10 minutes   Yield: 6-7 burgers

Another inspired recipe from Chef Davide, these "burgers" are really scrumptious. As Chef Davide suggested to us, you must serve these with the Cabbage Salad (page 132) and a drizzle of Basil Oil (page 159). You will fall in love just like we did with the fresh flavors and simple preparation of what now is a staple meal in our house.

1 pound white fish such as cod or tilapia, finely chopped

¼ cup sun-dried tomatoes, minced

3 tablespoons white onion, minced

1 tablespoon Italian parsley, minced

2 tablespoons chives, minced

1 cup carrots, shredded

1 tablespoon Garlic Oil (page 158)

Pinch or two of sea salt and black pepper

Basil Oil (page 159)

1. Preheat your oven to 300°F.

2. In a large mixing bowl, mix together the fish, sun-dried tomatoes, onion, parsley, chives, carrots, Garlic Oil, salt, and pepper.

3. Line a baking sheet with parchment paper.

4. Using a 3-inch ring mold as a guide, make the fish mixture into burgers, and space them evenly on the parchment paper.

5. Bake for 7-10 minutes, and serve the burgers with Cabbage Salad (page 132) and drizzled with the Basil Oil (page 159).

Fish Fillets with Celery Cream

filetto di pesce su crema di sedano

Prep Time: 30 minutes   Cook Time: 15 minutes   Serves: 4

Chef Clelia of Lucitta is a culinary genius in the making. Her innovative and fun style was refreshing, and her food, delightful. This is my version of one of the first dishes she made for us. I'll never forget watching Clelia at work. She is a powerful, bright, intuitive woman, working hard to make her dreams a reality and provide amazing service to the tourists who swarm her restaurant during the busy season on Sardinia. You must go visit her at Lucitta and let her work her culinary magic for you. You will not regret it.

CELERY CREAM

1½ cups water

½ teaspoon sea salt

8 celery stalks with leaves, diced

½ cup leeks, diced

1 garlic clove

2 tablespoons extra virgin olive oil

FISH

2 tablespoons butter or ghee per fish fillet

4 3-4 ounce fish fillets such as halibut or ahi tuna

Sea salt and pepper

¼ cup white wine per fish filet

GARNISH

Baby salad greens

Radishes, sliced

Extra virgin olive oil

Lemon wedges

Salt and pepper to taste

1. In a large saucepan, make the celery cream by cooking the water, salt, celery, leeks, garlic and olive oil over medium-high heat.

2. Simmer the veggies for 5-7 minutes or until tender.

3. Remove the pan from the heat, and add the olive oil.

4. Using a handheld immersion blender or a food processor, blend the mixture until smooth.

5. Season to taste with additional sea salt, if desired, and set the celery cream aside.

6. In a large skillet, heat the butter or ghee over medium-high heat.

7. Season both sides of the fish fillets with salt and pepper, and sear for 4-5 minutes per side in the hot pan.

8. Add the white wine to the hot pan with the fish and gently swirl the wine in the pan and spoon over the fish.

9. Remove the fish from the pan.

10. Serve the fish on top of the Celery Cream and garnished with baby salad greens, sliced radishes, a drizzle of extra virgin olive oil, lemon wedges, and more salt and pepper, if desired.

Baked Fish with Sweet Potatoes

pesce al forno con patate dolci

Prep Time: 45 minutes   Cook Time: 1 hour   Serves: 5-6

Back to the Marche region and to that little slice of heaven that was Chef Virginio's Osteria Da Gustin. It was almost a spiritual experience to be with Chef Virginio and his family while they worked to keep the family business alive. Not only are they keeping it alive, they are creating a legacy. The warmth and love that oozes from the tiny Osteria brings in people from all around the Marche region. I will be back there someday, because a piece of my heart will always be in that tiny village nestled in the beautiful hills of green.

4-5 cups white sweet potatoes, peeled and cubed

5-7 fresh or dry bay leaves

3 pounds white fish fillets, such as cod, cut into 3-4 inch long fillets

Sea salt and black pepper to taste

3-4 garlic cloves, minced

2 tablespoons sage leaves, minced

2 tablespoons fresh rosemary, minced

2 cups cherry tomatoes, cut into quarters

1 cup cured black olives with pits

¼ cup melted lard, butter, or ghee

Lemon wedges for garnish

Extra virgin olive oil

1. Preheat your oven to 350°F.

2. Meanwhile, fill a large soup pot halfway with water, and bring it to a boil over high heat.

3. Drop the cubed potatoes into the water, and cook them for 5-7 minutes so that they start to become tender but are still firm.

4. Drain the potatoes immediately, and set them aside.

5. Spread the bay leaves evenly on the bottom of a 9" X 13" baking dish.

6. Place the cod pieces on top of the bay leaves and sprinkle the fish with sea salt and black pepper.

7. In a bowl, mix together the garlic, sage, and rosemary, and sprinkle half of the mixture over the fish.

8. Evenly spread the potatoes over the fish, followed by the tomatoes and whole olives.

9. Sprinkle the remaining herb mixture over the top of the entire dish.

10. Drizzle on the melted lard, butter, or ghee, cover the dish tightly with foil, and bake in the oven for 35-40 minutes or until the potatoes are fork tender and the fish easily flakes apart.

11. Serve with lemon wedges and drizzle each serving with a little bit of extra virgin olive oil.

Fish Fillets with Green Beans
& Potato Cream

filetto di pesce con piselli e purea di patate

Prep Time: 1 hour   Cook Time: 30 minutes   Serves: 4-5

Chef Roberto made for us a delicious cream with white potatoes and no flour—just the potato starch for thickness and a few other key ingredients. Paired with crispy green beans and a fresh fish fillet, this was a gourmet meal turned comfort food, executed quickly and with precision. Here is my take on our beloved chef's creation. Make this for your next special occasion, and you will be sure to impress.

POTATO CREAM

1 tablespoon duck fat, butter, or ghee

½ cup shallots, finely diced

1 leek, finely diced

4 cups white sweet potatoes, diced

2 tablespoons extra virgin olive oil

Sea salt to taste

GREEN BEANS

3 ounces pancetta, diced

3 cups green beans, diced

2 garlic cloves, minced

1 tablespoon basil, freshly minced

Sea salt to taste

FISH

1 tablespoon lard, butter, or ghee per fish fillet

4 fish fillets (3-4 ounces each) such as halibut or ahi tuna

Sea salt

GARNISH

Extra virgin olive oil

½ cup fresh basil, diced

Lemon wedges

1. In a large sauté pan, heat the duck fat, butter, or ghee over medium heat.

2. Add the shallots and leek, and sauté them for 5-7 minutes.

3. Add the diced sweet potatoes, and sauté for another 5-7 minutes.

4. Add enough water to just cover the potatoes, and simmer uncovered until the potatoes are fork tender and the liquid is almost gone.

5. Remove the sauté pan from the heat, and add the extra virgin olive oil.

6. Using a handheld immersion blender, blend the vegetables until completely smooth. You can also remove the contents of the pan into a food processor, blender, or Vitamix for blending.

7. Season the potato cream to taste with sea salt, and set it aside.

8. Heat a large separate skillet over medium high-heat, and add the pancetta. Cook the pancetta until it starts to brown.

9. Add the green beans, and sauté for 5 minutes.

10. Add the garlic, and cook for another 4-5 minutes.

11. Add the fresh basil and sea salt to taste, and mix well.

12. Remove the skillet from the heat, cover to keep it warm, and set it aside.

13. Finally, prepare the fish. In a large skillet, heat 1 tablespoon of lard, butter, or ghee per fish fillet over medium-high heat.

14. Before placing the fish in the skillet, season each fillet on all sides with sea salt. Then, add them to the hot skillet, and sear them for 3-4 minutes per side, depending on the thickness of the fillets. The fish should be browned on all sides but still opaque in the middle. When done, remove the fish from the skillet, and set the fillets aside.

15. To plate the fish, place about ¼ cup of potato cream on each plate, top with a fish fillet, and serve with a side of green beans either next to or on top of the fish.

16. Garnish the fish with a drizzle of extra virgin olive oil, a sprinkle of freshly diced basil, and a lemon wedge.

Red Snapper with Orange Sauce

dentice in salsa all'arancia

Prep Time: 10 minutes   Cook Time: 10 minutes   Serves: 4-5

I love sweet and savory together, and this recipe does not disappoint in that regard. I learned this technique from Chef Andrea. In the kitchen back at home, we tweaked his idea to fit our taste. I love the added spice from the red pepper flakes paired with orange glaze and the fresh fish.

FISH

4-5 red snapper fillets (4 ounces each)

Sea salt

SAUCE

(Note that the amounts are per fish fillet, so if you cook 4 fillets, you must quadruple the sauce ingredients)

2 cups orange juice

1 teaspoon lemon juice

2 garlic cloves, minced

1 tablespoon shallots, minced

1-2 teaspoons red pepper flakes (more or less to taste)

1. Season each fish fillet on both sides with sea salt, and set them aside.

2. In a large skillet, heat the lard, butter, or ghee over medium-high heat.

3. Once the oil is hot, add the fish fillets, and cook them for 1 minute per side.

4. Add the orange juice and lemon juice, cover the pan, and poach the fish in the liquid for 3-4 minutes or until the fish flakes easily.

5. Remove the fillets from the pan, and set them aside.

6. Add the garlic, shallots, and red pepper flakes to the liquid in the pan. Simmer the sauce, whisking occasionally, over medium-high heat until the sauce is reduced by half and begins to thicken.

7. Pour the sauce over the cooked fish fillets, and serve immediately.

Shrimp with Fennel Cream
gamberi con crema di finocchi

Prep Time: 45 minutes   Cook Time: 30 minutes   Serves: 4-5

Here's another one of Chef Clelia's creations, simplified so that the home cook can accomplish the same flavors. Clelia originally made this meal by using a meat mallet to gently flatten three raw prawns until paper thin and wrapping them around the finely diced and cooked veggies. Then, she wrapped the whole thing in a special plastic that can be heated and cooked them at a very low temperature in the oven, serving them like little "dumplings" with a fennel cream sauce. Recreating this dish would be frustrating for the home cook, so I took the flavors of the original dish and simplified the process. The fennel cream is so light and delicious. Be sure to experiment and serve it with other seafood of your choice as well.

FENNEL CREAM

1 large fennel bulb, diced (approximately 1 cup)

2 small leeks, diced (1 cup)

1 garlic bulb, halved

1 cup Vegetable Broth (page 138)

2 tablespoons extra virgin olive oil

Sea salt to taste

SHRIMP

2 tablespoons butter or ghee

1 small carrot, finely diced

3 celery stalks, finely diced

½ cup leeks, finely diced

1-2 garlic cloves, minced

1 pound shrimp, shells removed and deveined

2 tablespoons white wine

2 tablespoons extra virgin olive oil

Salt and pepper to taste

Lemon juice to taste

1. Prepare the fennel cream by placing the diced fennel bulb, garlic, and leeks in a large saucepan.

2. Add the Vegetable Broth, and bring it to a simmer over medium-high heat. Cook until the fennel and leeks are tender, about 15 minutes.

3. Remove the pan from the heat, and add the extra virgin olive oil.

4. Using a handheld immersion blender, purée the vegetables and broth until smooth. You can also remove the contents of the pan into a food processor, blender, or Vitamix for blending.

5. Season the purée to taste with sea salt, and set it aside.

6. Next, prepare the shrimp. In a large skillet, heat the butter or ghee over medium heat.

7. Add the carrot, celery, and leeks, and sauté them until they are tender.

8. Add the garlic, and sauté just until fragrant.

9. Add the shrimp and the white wine, and turn the heat to medium-high. Sauté for another 3-4 minutes or until the shrimp are pink and tender.

10. Remove the skillet from the heat, and stir in the olive oil, salt, pepper, and lemon juice to taste.

11. Serve the shrimp on top of the fennel cream.

Stuffed Calamari
calamari ripieni

Prep Time: 30 minutes   Cook Time: 10 minutes   Serves: 3-4

This is a fun recipe of Chef Clelia's that you can make with the whole family. So, take your time with this one, and enjoy the moment. Relax, slow down, laugh together, and live the Italian lifestyle for an afternoon, eating real food and living life to its fullest.

Red Bell Pepper Sauce (page 166)

1 pound whole calamari

1 red bell pepper

1 yellow bell pepper

1 zucchini

1 carrot

2 tablespoons fresh rosemary, minced

2 tablespoons fresh sage, minced

1 tablespoon sea salt

2 tablespoons lard, butter, or ghee

1. Make the Red Bell Pepper Sauce.

2. If necessary, clean the calamari, and reserve the tentacles for sauce or stock.

3. Cut the bell peppers, zucchini, and carrot into long stick pieces all the same length. They should be a bit longer than the bodies of the calamari.

4. Place the veggies in a steamer basket, and steam them for 3-4 minutes or until still crisp but a bit tender. Set them aside to cool.

5. Once the veggies are cool enough to handle, stuff the bodies of the calamari with even amounts of the veggies.

6. In a medium-sized bowl, mix together the rosemary, sage, and sea salt.

7. Roll the stuffed calamari in the spice mixture to coat.

8. In a large skillet, heat the lard, butter, or ghee over medium heat. Add the stuffed calamari to the pan, and cook, turning over often, for 3-4 minutes or until the calamari is tender. The calamari will go from translucent to opaque; stop cooking when it becomes opaque. Be careful not to overcook; you may need to adjust the cooking time depending on the size of your calamari.

9. Slice the calamari into 2-inch rings, and serve it with the Red Bell Pepper Sauce (page 166).

Note: If you opt to clean the calamari yourself instead of buying pre-cleaned, the prep time increases from 30 minutes to 1 hour.

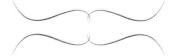

Stuffed Chicken
pollo ripieno

Prep Time: 45 minutes   Cook Time: 35 minutes   Serves: 4-5

Red Bell Pepper Sauce (page 166)

1 red bell pepper

1 yellow bell pepper

1 zucchini

1 carrot

2 tablespoons fresh rosemary, minced

2 tablespoons fresh sage, minced

1 tablespoon sea salt

2 chicken breasts, halved

2 tablespoons lard, butter, or ghee

1. Make the Red Bell Pepper Sauce.

2. Preheat your oven to 350°F.

3. Cut the bell peppers, zucchini, and carrot into long stick pieces all the same length. They should be a bit longer than the chicken breasts, if possible.

4. Place the veggies in a steamer basket, and steam them for 3-4 minutes or until still crisp but a bit tender. Set them aside to cool.

5. Meanwhile, in a medium-sized bowl, mix together the rosemary, sage, and sea salt.

6. Lay the chicken breast halves between 2 pieces of plastic wrap, and using a meat mallet, pound the chicken breasts until they are about ¼-inch in thickness.

7. Place about 3 pieces of each vegetable in the center of each flattened chicken breast half, and sprinkle the chicken and veggies with a little bit of the herb mixture.

8. Roll the chicken tightly around the veggies, and secure them with toothpicks.

9. Roll the stuffed chicken breasts in the herb mixture, and set them aside.

10. In a large skillet, heat the lard, butter, or ghee over medium-high heat.

11. Once the pan is hot, add the stuffed chicken to the pan, and brown it on all sides.

12. Transfer the chicken to the oven, and bake it for 15 minutes or until the juices run clear.

13. Slice the chicken into 2-inch rings, and serve it with the Red Bell Pepper Sauce (page 166).

Herbed Chicken with Pancetta

pollo alle erbette con pancetta

Prep Time: 45 minutes   Cook Time: 1 hour   Serves: 4

Holy cow! Or maybe I should say Holy Chicken! Damon, Angela, John, and I sat in silence while we ate this chicken. It was a culinary experience we'll never forget –chicken brought to a whole new level. Chef Virginio, thank you for showing me how to make this recipe. I did not change a thing. This is all you! I'm forever grateful for meeting you and your beautiful family. You changed my worldview forever and fed me some of the most delicious food I've ever eaten. Now, you, my readers, can enjoy the experience, too! Serve with the Italian Roasted Sweet Potatoes (page 128).

1 whole chicken

3 tablespoons fresh sage, minced

3 tablespoons fresh rosemary, minced

3 tablespoons fresh bay leaves, minced

6 garlic cloves, minced

6 ounces pancetta or bacon, thinly sliced

Sea salt

Extra virgin olive oil

1. Preheat your oven to 375°F.

2. Rinse the chicken, and remove the giblets.\

3. Dry the chicken thoroughly with paper towels, sprinkle the entire chicken lightly with sea salt, and set it aside.

4. Meanwhile, mince together the sage, rosemary, bay leaves, and garlic.

5. Follow the photo instructions to prepare the chicken.

6. Drizzle the top of the chicken with extra virgin olive oil.

7. Place the chicken with the pancetta side up on a baking sheet, and bake, uncovered, for 30 minutes.

8. Turn the chicken over, and roast it for an additional 30 minutes or until the chicken reaches an internal temperature of 165°F.

9. Remove the poultry needles or toothpicks and cut the chicken into quarters, and serve.

Chicken Preparation for Herbed Chicken with Pancetta

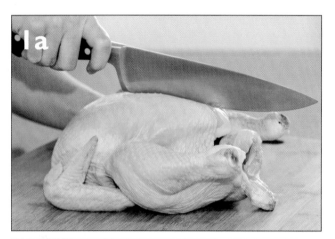

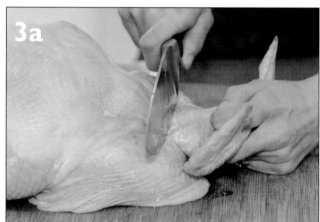

1. Place the chicken on a cutting board breast side up and make a cut down the middle so that you can open the chicken to see the cavity but do NOT cut entirely in half.

2. Turn the chicken over cut side down, grab the wings, bring them up above the body of the chicken and press them down flat.

3. Using the blade of your knife, strike the bottom of the wings closest to the body, breaking the bones in order to be able to lay the wings out flat in front of the chicken's body.

4. Cover the entire chicken with plastic wrap and using a meat mallet, pound the breasts and legs of the chicken to flatten.

5. Remove the plastic wrap and season the skin side of the chicken with sea salt.

6. Turn the chicken over to expose the cavity and spread open and flat and season the entire cavity of the chicken with sea salt and the herb mixture.

7. Place an even layer of pancetta or bacon over the herb mixture and secure with toothpicks or poultry needles.

8. Cut the chicken in half next to the spine lengthwise.

Chicken or Rabbit Stew

spiedini di pollo spiedini di coniglio

Prep Time: 45 minutes   Cook Time: 30 minutes   Serves: 5

The mixture of herbs, onions, and capers will make this authentic stew a hit the whole family will love. As mentioned in the ingredient resource guide, you can order rabbit from US Wellness Meats, or you can also make it with chicken if you're less adventurous. The flavors intensify and improve the following day so this dish also makes excellent leftovers for lunch.

2 tablespoons lard, duck fat, butter, or ghee

1 medium yellow onion, diced

4 celery stalks, diced

4 carrots, diced

3 garlic cloves, cut in half

2 pounds rabbit cut into bite-sized pieces or 2 pounds boneless chicken thighs, breasts, or a combination of both, cut into bite-sized pieces

⅓ cup dry red wine

½ cup sun-dried tomatoes, diced

2 bay leaves

1 tablespoon fresh sage, minced

1 tablespoon fresh rosemary, minced

3 tablespoons capers

1 15-ounce can tomato sauce

3 tablespoons extra virgin olive oil

Sea salt and black pepper to taste

1. In a large skillet, heat the lard, duck fat, butter, or ghee over medium heat. Add the onion, celery, and carrots, and sauté for 5-7 minutes.

2. Turn the heat to medium-high, and add the garlic and rabbit or chicken pieces. Sauté until the meat starts to brown, about 4-5 minutes.

3. Add the red wine to the hot pan, and simmer for 3-4 minutes.

4. Add the sun-dried tomatoes, bay leaves, sage, rosemary, capers, and tomato sauce to the pan. Mix well, turn the heat to medium-low, and simmer for another 12-15 minutes or until the chicken or rabbit is cooked all the way through.

5. Add the extra virgin olive oil to the pan, and season to taste with salt and pepper.

Chicken Marsala

pollo al marsala

Prep Time: 30 minutes   Cook Time: 30 minutes   Serves: 4-5

I don't have words for the deliciousness of this recipe. Just trust me! Make it, and see for yourself. All of our testers agreed that it's "top of the list" good!

2 boneless, skinless chicken breasts, halved

Sea salt and black pepper to taste

4 tablespoons duck fat, butter or ghee, divided

3 cups mushrooms, sliced

1 cup Marsala wine

1 cup Chicken Broth (page 141)

1 sprig rosemary

1. Place the chicken breast halves on a large cutting board, and cover them with plastic wrap. Using a meat mallet, gently pound the chicken breast halves until they are approximately ¼-inch thick.

2. Season both sides of the flattened chicken breasts with sea salt and pepper.

3. In a large skillet, heat 2 tablespoons of the duck fat, butter or ghee over medium-high heat.

4. Once the pan is hot, add the chicken breasts, and sear them for 3-4 minutes per side or until golden brown. Remove the chicken breasts from the pan, and set them aside.

5. In the same pan, add the remaining 2 tablespoons of duck fat, butter or ghee. Once melted, add the mushrooms, and sauté for 4-5 minutes.

6. Add the Marsala wine, and bring it to a simmer, stirring occasionally. Cook the mushrooms and wine together for 3-4 minutes.

7. Add the Chicken Broth and sprig of rosemary, and stir.

8. Add the chicken back to the pan, cover, and cook for an additional 8-10 minutes or until the chicken is cooked all the way through.

9. Remove the chicken from the sauce, and slice it into strips, if desired. Serve the chicken topped with the Marsala sauce.

Chicken with Fig Sauce

pollo con salsa ai fichi

Prep Time: 1 hour   Cook Time: 30 minutes   Serves: 4-5

What's nice about this dish is that it uses dried figs, so even if figs are not in season, you can still enjoy this meal. Sweet from the figs, savory from the pancetta and pearl onions, it's like my brother said, "an Italian coq au vin." Enjoy!

2 boneless, skinless chicken breasts, halved

Salt and pepper to taste

6 tablespoons duck fat, butter or ghee, divided

8 ounces pancetta, diced

6 ounces pearl onions

¼ cup shallots

I cup Chicken Broth (page 141)

¼ cup balsamic vinegar

I cup dried figs, chopped and rehydrated (to rehydrate the figs, cover with hot water and let sit on the counter until soft; approximately 30 minutes to I hour)

I teaspoon fresh oregano, minced

2 teaspoons fresh thyme, minced

1. Salt and pepper the chicken breasts.

2. In a large skillet, heat the 4 tablespoons duck fat, butter, or ghee over medium heat. Add the chicken breasts, and sear for 4-5 minutes per side or until browned. Remove the chicken from the pan, and set it aside.

3. In the same skillet, melt the other 2 tablespoons duck fat, butter, or ghee. Add the pancetta, pearl onions, and shallots, and cook until the pancetta is crispy and the onions and shallots are almost fully cooked.

4. Add the Chicken Broth, balsamic vinegar, figs, oregano, thyme to the pan, and simmer for 4-5 minutes.

5. Add the seared chicken breasts to the pan, and cover them with sauce.

6. Cover the pan, and cook until the chicken is done and the juices run clear, turning the chicken breasts over periodically.

7. You can either serve the chicken breast pieces whole or sliced and topped with plenty of the sauce.

Slow Cooked Pork Belly
with Pomegranate Reduction

pancetta di maiale cotta a bassa temperatura con riduzione di melagrana

Prep Time: 30 minutes   Cook Time: 7-9 hours   Serves: 4-5

Chef Roberto, thank you for making me pork belly. My taste buds will never be the same! This is my rendition of his phenomenal creation. Ask your butcher for pork belly if they don't already stock it or check www.eatwild.com to find a pasture-raised pork provider in your area. After trying this recipe, you will most likely become a pork belly lover like me!

4 pounds pork belly

Sea salt and black pepper

2 tablespoons honey

2 fresh sprigs rosemary

1 cup pomegranate juice

2 tablespoons duck fat or lard

1. Using a knife, score the skin side of the pork belly by cutting about ¼-inch deep into the skin, making sure your knife reaches the fat underneath the skin and cut at a diagonal. Continue making the cuts about half an inch apart.

2. Season all sides of the pork belly with sea salt and black pepper, and place the pork in a slow cooker, making sure the skin side is facing up.

3. Drizzle the top of the pork belly with the honey, and place the sprigs of rosemary on top of the meat.

4. Cover the slow cooker, and cook on low for 7-9 hours.

5. Remove the pork belly from the slow cooker, and discard the rosemary.

6. In a small saucepan, add the pomegranate juice, and bring it to a simmer over medium-high heat.

7. Stirring often, reduce the pomegranate juice until it is at a maple syrup consistency. Remove it from the heat, and set it aside.

8. In a large skillet, heat the duck fat or lard over medium-high heat. Once the pan is hot, add the slow cooked pork belly, and sear it for 2-3 minutes on each side.

9. Cut the pork belly into the same number of portions as people you will be serving, and drizzle the portions with the pomegranate reduction before serving.

10. If your reduction becomes too sticky and/or thick, add more juice, place it back over the medium-high heat, and whisk it until it reaches the desired consistency.

DOLCI

Dessert

Poached Pears

pere in camicia

Prep Time: 20 minutes   Cook Time: 10 minutes   Serves: 6-8

We ate delicious poached pears twice while in Italy. Although this version has much less sugar than the typical Italian dessert, it's still just as tasty. You can use either coconut milk or heavy cream for the whipped cream—both ways are divine! My kids love this dessert, and I love to make it for them. It's easy, tasty, and fun!

4 bosc pears, peeled, halved, and cored

Organic grape juice, enough to cover the pears

1 13.5-ounce can full-fat coconut milk, placed in the refrigerator overnight or 2 cups heavy cream

1½ ounces dark chocolate, melted

Fresh mint for garnish

1. In a large saucepan, cover the pears with grape juice.

2. Bring the grape juice to a simmer over medium heat, then turn the heat to medium-low. Simmer for 7-10 minutes or until the pears are fork tender and take on the color of the grape juice.

3. With a slotted spoon, gently remove the pears from the grape juice and set them aside.

4. Open the can of cold coconut milk, and scoop only the cream at the top into a small mixing bowl. Save the coconut water for later use.

5. Using a handheld mixer, beat the coconut cream on high until it's the consistency of whipped cream, and set it aside.

6. In a double boiler, melt the dark chocolate.

7. To serve the poached pears, place a small spoonful of the whipped coconut cream on a plate, top with a poached pear half, and drizzle it with the melted dark chocolate. Garnish with the fresh mint.

Tiramisù

Prep Time: 1 hour   Cook Time: 6-8 minutes (for the lady fingers)   Serves: 7-10

WARNING, as I said before, this is not Paleo, because it does require cheese! You can't make tiramisu without mascarpone, so if you tolerate a little dairy from time to time, this dessert is truly a special treat. The ladyfingers are grain-free, so there's no need to worry about that. Personally, when I kick up my heels and enjoy some cheese, this Tiramisù is what I make.

6 eggs, separated

½ cup honey

8 ounces mascarpone cheese

Lady Fingers (page 256)

1 cup brewed espresso

2 tablespoons Marsala wine, optional

Cocoa powder for garnish

1. Separate the eggs, and place the whites in a medium-sized mixing bowl. Place the yolks in a large mixing bowl.

2. Using a handheld mixer, beat the egg whites into stiff peaks. Clean the beaters.

3. Add the honey to the egg yolks, and beat them together until smooth and creamy.

4. Add the mascarpone to the honey and egg yolks, and blend with the handheld mixer.

5. Using a spoon, fold the egg whites half at a time into the mascarpone mixture.

6. Place the mixture in the refrigerator.

7. Prepare the Lady Fingers.

8. In a small bowl, mix together the espresso and the Marsala wine.

9. To assemble the tiramisu, place a big spoonful of the cream (the mascarpone mixture) into the bottom of a dessert cup. Soak 2 of the lady fingers into the espresso and wine mixture for about 30 seconds, and place them on top of the cream. Top with another scoop of the cream, and sprinkle the top with cocoa powder.

10. Serve immediately, or chill if desired, before serving.

Tip: This dessert also freezes well so you can make a batch ahead of time and pull it out of the freezer a couple of hours before it's time to serve.

Lady Fingers
savoiardi

Prep Time: 20 minutes   Cook Time: 6-8 minutes   Serves: 10-12 lady fingers

You can dip these in espresso for a treat, but they're also fun and tasty as-is. My kids like to help pipe these out and watch them bake!

4 eggs, separated

¼ cup blanched almond flour

¼ cup coconut flour, sifted

2 tablespoons arrowroot flour

½ teaspoon baking powder

2 tablespoons honey

1 tablespoon pure vanilla extract

1. Preheat your oven to 400°F.

2. Line a baking sheet with parchment paper, and set it aside.

3. Separate the eggs, placing the whites into a large bowl and the yolks into a small bowl.

4. Using a handheld mixer, beat the egg whites into stiff peaks. Clean the beaters.

5. In a medium-sized mixing bowl, mix the almond flour, coconut flour, arrowroot flour, and baking powder together.

6. Into the small mixing bowl, add the honey and vanilla extract to the egg yolks, and mix them together with a handheld mixer.

7. Add the egg yolk mixture to the dry ingredients, and blend them together until smooth.

8. Using a spoon, fold the egg whites into the egg yolk mixture.

9. Fill a pastry bag with the dough, and pipe out 4-inch long lady fingers evenly spaced onto the parchment paper-lined baking sheet.

10. Bake in the oven for 6-8 minutes or until the lady fingers are golden brown.

Tip: If you do not have a pastry bag, fill a gallon zip lock bag with the dough and cut off a bottom corner of the bag making a dime sized hole and pipe the dough through the homemade pastry bag!

Strawberries & Prosecco
fragole al prosecco

Prep Time: 45 minutes   Serves: 4-5

This is such a romantic dessert. Prosecco bubbling over ripe strawberries has "night alone with your sweetheart" written all over it. Save this for that special celebratory occasion. Big Carlo shared this recipe with us, and I'm so glad he did. It's fun and easy but very special.

3 cups strawberries, sliced

3 tablespoons honey, optional

1 bottle of Prosecco or sparkling apple cider

1. In a medium-sized mixing bowl, drizzle the sliced strawberries with the honey, and stir well to coat the strawberries.

2. Place the strawberries in the refrigerator for at least 30 minutes.

3. Scoop a large spoonful of strawberries into each of 4-5 dessert cups.

4. Right before you serve the strawberries, pour enough Prosecco or sparkling apple cider over them to cover. Eat with a spoon.

Panna Cotta

Prep Time: 20 minutes   Cook Time: 15 minutes +3 hours to chill   Serves: 6-10

Creamy, a little bit sweet, and satisfying– I love this dessert and love how it was served in Italy with fresh berries on top.

6 tablespoons cold water

2 packets unflavored gelatin

2 cups heavy cream or canned, full-fat coconut milk

½ cup honey

1 tablespoon pure vanilla extract

OPTIONAL

Blueberries, blackberries, or raspberries

1. In a large mixing bowl, add the cold water, and sprinkle the gelatin over the top. Let it sit for 10 minutes.

2. Meanwhile, in a saucepan, add the heavy cream or coconut milk, and cook over medium heat until hot but not yet boiling.

3. Remove the heavy cream or coconut milk from the heat, and add the honey and pure vanilla extract to the pan. Whisk well until the honey is melted.

4. Pour the very warm cream mixture over the gelatin, and gently whisk until the gelatin is completely dissolved.

5. Pour the liquid into custard cups, small muffin tins, or dessert cups, and refrigerate for 3 hours or until the Panna Cotta is firm.

6. Serve topped with mixed berries, if desired.

Almond Cookies

biscotti alle mandorle

Prep Time: 30 minutes   Cook Time: 8-10 minutes   Yield: 24 cookies

The classic Italian almond cookie is often eaten for breakfast, but I don't advise that strategy. These are treats like all of the other desserts in this section and are the perfect end to your Italian meal or a fun afternoon project with the kiddos.

4 egg whites

1 cup almond butter

1½ cups blanched almond flour

⅓ cup honey

½ teaspoon almond extract

¼ cup sliced almonds

1. Preheat your oven to 350°F.

2. Line a baking sheet with parchment paper, and set it aside.

3. In a large mixing bowl, beat the egg whites to stiff peaks with a handheld mixer.

4. In a separate medium-sized mixing bowl, make the cookie dough by adding the almond butter, almond flour, honey, and almond extract. Blend the ingredients well with a handheld mixer.

5. Using a spoon, fold the egg whites into the cookie dough.

6. Drop heaping tablespoons of dough onto the parchment paper, making sure to leave about two inches between each cookie.

7. Press a few almond slices into the top of each cookie.

8. Bake the cookies in the preheated oven for 8-10 minutes.

Amaretto Zabaglione

zabaione agli amaretti

Prep Time: Overnight for chilling   Cook Time: 5 minutes   Serves: 5-6

If you want to be fancy and impress your guests, this is the dessert for you! I suggest doing a trial run, however, before you commit to making these for friends. This recipe can be a little tricky, so read the directions carefully and follow them to a T. If you do, you should be fine!

6 egg yolks

2 tablespoons almond liquor or 1 tablespoon almond extract

¼ cup honey

½ cup coconut cream or ½ cup heavy cream (for the coconut cream, place a can of coconut milk in the refrigerator overnight so that the cream rises to the top of the can)

1. Add the egg yolks, almond liquor or almond extract, and ¼ cup honey to the top of a double boiler and whisk together.

2. Fill the bottom of the double boiler about ½ full with water and turn the heat to medium high.

3. When the water is very hot but NOT boiling, add the top of the double boiler and whisk the egg mixture constantly for 10 minutes or until the mixture becomes frothy and pale and triples in volume.

4. Remove from the heat and set aside.

5. In a small bowl add the cream from the coconut milk or the heavy cream and using a hand held mixer, beat the coconut cream or whipped cream into thick whipped cream.

6. Mix gently with the egg yolk mixture and serve immediately in small custard cups with more whipped cream on top and fresh berries if desired.

7. Servings should be small—this is a very rich dessert.

ANTIPASTI

76
Green Olives with Sun-Dried Tomatoes

78
Turkey Breast Antipasto

80
Stuffed Squash Blossoms

82
Fried Squash Blossoms

84
Italian Shrimp Cocktail

86
Chopped Chicken Salad

88
Vegetable Quiche

90
Mushroom Antipasto

92
Zucchini Quiche

94
Italian Pickled Vegetables

96
Roasted Garlic

98
Salmon Carpaccio

99
Tomato Bruschetta

100
Artichoke Bruschetta

101
Mixed Antipasto

102
Caponata

104
Stuffed Mushrooms

106
Radicchio with Pancetta Dressing

108
Drunken Cauliflower

110
Artichokes with Salsa Verde

PIZZE

115

Pizza Crust

116

Pizza 1
Extra virgin olive oil, sliced tomato, thinly sliced garlic cloves, fresh oregano leaves, sprinkle of sea salt

117

Pizza 2
Tomato sauce, sprinkle of dry oregano, thinly sliced ham, sliced mushrooms, sliced artichoke hearts, chopped kalamata olives

117

Pizza 3
Tomato sauce, sprinkle of dry oregano, thinly sliced mushrooms, anchovies, thinly sliced ham, sliced black olives

118

Pizza 4
Tomato sauce, arugula, thinly sliced prosciutto

118

Pizza 5
Pesto Sauce, thinly sliced mushrooms, thinly sliced eggplant, cooked and crumbled mild Italian sausage, tomato slices

119

Pizza 6
Tomato sauce, thinly sliced ham, thinly sliced crimini mushrooms, 1 egg, basil leaves

119

Pizza 7
Tomato sauce, sliced zucchini, thinly sliced eggplant, spinach leaves, thinly sliced purple onions, thinly sliced red bell peppers, cooked and crumbled mild Italian sausage, drizzle of extra virgin olive oil

120

Pizza 8
Extra virgin olive oil, prosciutto, sun-dried tomatoes, sliced black olives, basil leaves, thinly sliced purple onions

120

Pizza 9
Extra virgin olive oil, sliced artichoke hearts, sun-dried tomatoes, cooked and crumbled spicy Italian sausage, basil leaves

121

Pizza 10
Tomato sauce, cooked and crumbled mild Italian sausage, thinly sliced ham, diced and cooked pancetta, capers, thinly sliced fennel

PRIMI PIATTI

First Courses, Sauces, Side Dishes & Soups

124 Noodles

126 Sweet Potato Soufflé

128 Italian Roasted Sweet Potatoes

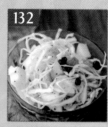
130 Mushrooms with Tomato

132 Cabbage Salad

134 Egg with Asparagus

136 Eggplant Parmesan

138 Vegetable Broth

140 Beef Broth

141 Chicken Broth

142 Pumpkin Cream with Prawns

144 Mussels & Clams Soup

146 Vegetable Soup

148 Fish Soup

150 Meatball & Escarole Soup

152 Minestrone Soup

154 Creamy Carrot Fennel Soup

156 Herb Mixture

157 Balsamic Reduction

158 Garlic Oil

159 Basil Oil

160 Béchamel Sauce

162 Basic Tomato Sauce

164 Tomato Cream

166 Red Bell Pepper Sauce

167 Pesto

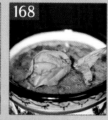
168 Creamy Sun-Dried Tomato Pesto

169 Sun-Dried Tomato Pesto

170 Gnocchi

172 Zucchini & Prosciutto Sauce

174

176

178

180

182

184

Red Clam Sauce

White Clam Sauce

Puttanesca Sauce

Spicy Sausage Spaghetti

Sarah's Spaghetti Carbonara

Classic Bolognese

186

188

190

192

194

196

Baked "Ziti"

Butter & Gold

Garlic Sauce

Calamari & Spinach Sauce

Sausage & Fennel Sauce

Mushroom "Risotto"

198

"Risotto" alla Milanese

SECONDI PIATTI

Main Dishes

202

204

206

208

210

212

Lasagna

Mushroom Meatballs with Easy Tomato Sauce

Meatballs & Spinach with Béchamel Sauce

Lamb with Aromatic Herbs

Lamb with Lemon & Eggs

Steak with Artichokes

216

218

220

222

224

226

Beef, Lamb, or Mutton Stew

Beef or Mutton Fillet with Pomegranate Reduction & Spring Salad

Steak with Savory Onions and Grapes

Ossobuco

Fish Burgers

Fish Fillets with Celery Cream

228
Baked Fish with Sweet Potatoes

230
Fish Fillets with Green Beans & Potato Cream

232
Red Snapper with Orange Sauce

234
Shrimp with Fennel Cream

236
Stuffed Calamari

236
Stuffed Chicken

238
Herbed Chicken with Pancetta

242
Chicken or Rabbit Stew

244
Chicken Marsala

246
Chicken with Fig Sauce

248
Slow Cooked Pork Belly with Pomegranate Reduction

DOLCI

Dessert

252
Poached Pears

254
Tiramisù

256
Lady Fingers

258
Strawberries & Prosecco

260
Panna Cotta

262
Almond Cookies

264
Amaretto Zabaglione

INGREDIENT INDEX

CONVERSION TABLES

WEIGHT

US	Metric
¼ ounce	7 grams
½ ounce	15 grams
¾ ounce	20 grams
1 ounce	30 grams
8 ounces	225 grams
12 ounces	340 grams
16 ounces (1 pound)	455 grams

VOLUME

US	Metric
1 teaspoon	5 mL
1 tablespoon	15 mL
¼ cup	60 mL
⅓ cup	80 mL
½ cup	120 mL
⅔ cup	160 mL
¾ cup	180 mL
1 cup	240 mL
1 quart	950 mL

TEMPERATURE

Fahrenheit	Celsius
32°	0°
180°	82°
212°	100°
250°	120°
350°	175°
425°	220°
500°	260°